Prime Time 5/6
Language in Use

Georg Hellmayr
Stephan Waba

www.oebv.at

Table of contents

Vocabulary

Unit	Page	Title	PTT 5	PT 5	PT 6
1	4	Speaking English • The world speaks English	Unit 1	Unit 1	
2	7	It's my life • Identities – what next?	Unit 2	Unit 2	
3	10	Up and away	Unit 3		
4	13	Hobbies	Unit 4		
5	16	Fifteen minutes of fame • Media-mad	Unit 5	Unit 4	
6	19	Music	Unit 6	Unit 8	
7	22	Jobs	Unit 7	Unit 9	
8	25	Crime and suspense	Unit 8		
9	28	Australia	Unit 9	Unit 3	
10	31	Books	Unit 10	Unit 10	
11	34	Politics		Unit 5	
12	36	Strange realities		Unit 6	
13	38	Human rights		Unit 7	
14	40	Growing up			Unit 1
15	43	Multi-ethnic Britain			Unit 2
16	46	The Blue Planet			Unit 3
17	49	Making a difference			Unit 4
18	52	Globalisation			Unit 5
19	55	South Africa			Unit 6
20	58	The world of work			Unit 7
21	61	Famous speeches			Unit 8
22	64	Sports			Unit 9
23	67	Beauty and fashion trends			Unit 10

PTT 5 = Prime Time 5 Transition (ISBN 978-3-209-08063-9 | SBNR 165463)
PT 5 = Prime Time 5 (ISBN 978-3-209-06705-0 | SBNR 150124)
PT 6 = Prime Time 6 (ISBN 978-3-209-07159-0 | SBNR 155137)

Grammar

Unit	Page	Title	PTT 5	PT 5	PT 6
1	70	Present forms	Unit 1	Unit 2 Unit 4	Unit 1 Unit 4
2	72	Past forms	Unit 3	Unit 2	Unit 4
3	75	Present perfect and other past forms	Unit 3	Unit 2	Unit 4
4	78	Future forms	Unit 2	Unit 2	Unit 6
5	80	Modal verbs	Unit 5	Unit 6	
6	82	Conditional clauses	Unit 10	Unit 10	Unit 6
7	85	Passive voice	Unit 8	Unit 1	
8	87	Indirect speech	Unit 7	Unit 9	
9	90	Gerund and infinitives		Unit 7	
10	93	Participle constructions		Unit 4	Unit 2
11	95	Verbs and their meaning	Unit 7 Unit 9	Unit 3 Unit 4 Unit 9	
12	97	Nouns and articles			Unit 9
13	99	Comparison of adjectives	Unit 4 Unit 6	Unit 8	Unit 3
14	101	Adjectives and adverbs of manner and degree	Unit 6	Unit 8	
15	104	Prepositions and phrasal verbs			Unit 7
16	108	Word formation	Unit 8 Unit 9	Unit 6	Unit 3
17	110	Relative clauses	Unit 9	Unit 3	
18	112	Adverbial clauses	Unit 8		
	114	Unit 1–23 (Vocabulary) Key			
	121	Unit 1–18 (Grammar) Key			

🖱 You will need internet access to complete this task.

● This type of exercise introduces the formats of the *Standardisierte Reifeprüfung* and other standardised tests.

Vocabulary

Speaking English
The world speaks English

> **TIP**
> • Prime Time Transition 5: Unit 1 → S. 6
> • Prime Time 5: Unit 1 → S. 6

1 Language in use: Talking about your own language experience

You are going to read a text about Nelson, a 16-year-old teenager from Norway. Some words are missing from the text. Choose the correct answer (A, B, C or D) for each gap (1–10) in the text. Write your answers in the boxes provided. The first one (0) has been done for you.

My name is Nelson and I'm from Norway. My mother ... **(0)** is Norwegian, but I can speak English ... **(Q1)** as well because all ... **(Q2)** films on TV are in the original language. Some people might think that I am a ... **(Q3)** speaker of Swedish as well because my mother is from Sweden. My ... **(Q4)** of Swedish, however, is rather basic. At home we speak Norwegian. Only when we visit my grandmother in Örebro in Sweden, my mother speaks Swedish because this is the language she would speak with her mother. I can understand simple ... **(Q5)** but I can only speak a little. I can talk about familiar topics but I cannot answer questions spontaneously because I am so embarrassed when I ... **(Q6)** mistakes.

I have been learning English for almost six years now – in school I mean. Most of the things we learn at school I know from the internet or from television anyway.

On top of that I have just started learning Spanish, but I find it very difficult because it is so ... **(Q7)** from the languages I know. My aim is to speak Spanish fluently and to be able to ... **(Q8)** with everyday situations. We'll see how ... **(Q9)** I can get. At the moment I can only talk about my personal details. And I can follow recordings of simple dialogues but only if they are very ... **(Q10)**.

0	A	speech	B	speak	C	tongue	D	language
Q1	A	fluently	B	fluent	C	flowing	D	followed
Q2	A	strange	B	foreign	C	outlandish	D	peculiar
Q3	A	naive	B	national	C	indigenous	D	native
Q4	A	wisdom	B	knowledge	C	ability	D	domination
Q5	A	speaking	B	converse	C	speak	D	conversations
Q6	A	make	B	do	C	undergo	D	avoid
Q7	A	other	B	various	C	altered	D	different
Q8	A	coup	B	cope	C	coupe	D	cop
Q9	A	far	B	farther	C	further	D	forth
Q10	A	slowly	B	slower	C	slowed	D	slow

0	Q1	Q2	Q3	Q4	Q5	Q6	Q7	Q8	Q9	Q10
C	A	B	D	B	D	B	D	B	A	D

Speaking English • The world speaks English

2 Countries and languages

Which languages are spoken in the following countries?

1. Belgium: Belgian
2. Bosnia-Herzegovina: Bosnian
3. China: Chinese
4. Croatia: Croatian
5. the Czech Republic: Czech
6. Denmark: Danish
7. Finland: Finnisch
8. Greece: Greek
9. Hungary: Hungarian
10. Ireland: Irish
11. Italy: Italian
12. the Netherlands: Dutch
13. Poland: Polish
14. Romania (Rumania): Romanian
15. Russia: Russian
16. Serbia: Serbian
17. Slovakia: Slovak
18. Slovenia: Slovenian
19. Switzerland: Swiss
20. Turkey: Turkish

3 Finding synonyms: English study tips

Go through the text on English study tips and find alternatives for the words and phrases below.

Study tips by other learners help to improve your English. Some students set a goal for themselves every week and ask themselves what they want to learn. That way they decide what is most important to them at that point. Some have even started a learning diary where
5 they record all their plans and ideas. They also use it to check if they have achieved what they had planned.

Organising your materials is certainly one of the priorities. This makes it easier to go through your materials before you start working on a project, e.g. preparing a presentation.

10 Listening to a lot of English in your free time is also very important. If you can watch films in their original version, you can improve your pronunciation as well.

Subtitles may help to understand the sections that are too difficult for you.

15 When you buy books or magazines, you should pick books that are appropriate for your level of English. If you are not sure of your level, go for books that have been made a bit simpler.

1. get better: improve
2. aim: set a goal
3. try to find out: ask themselves
4. at that moment: That way
5. record of your learning efforts: learning diary
6. most important things: achieve
7. a talk about a topic (e.g. with visual elements): priorites
8. translations on a screen: presentation
9. suitable: important
10. simplified: appropriate

1 Speaking English • The world speaks English

4 Learning tips: Making suggestions, giving advice

You have read a lot about how to learn a foreign language. Surely you have also found out which methods and which strategies work best.

a) From the list below, choose ten possible strategies that could help your friend who wants to improve his/her English.

- collect linking words
- collect words in word fields
- do exercises more than once
- keep a learning diary
- listen to English radio programmes on the internet
- listen to songs and look up the lyrics on the internet
- make lists of synonyms
- organise your materials
- plan your learning activities well ahead of your tests
- read articles from English papers or magazines
- read texts about topics you are interested in
- revise new words and phrases regularly
- rewrite texts and adapt them
- set a goal for yourself
- study a simplified text
- study the grammar pages in your coursebook
- use index cards to study new words
- use a dictionary if you don't understand a word or phrase
- watch as many English films as you can
- watch videos with subtitles
- write down new words and phrases

b) Now use the ten strategies you have chosen and the phrases below to give advice to your friend.

Example:

| Couldn't you **collect** linking words? | **Collecting** linking words is worth a try. |

Phrases + infinitive	Phrases + *-ing* form
Couldn't you … ? Don't you think it is a good idea to … ? If I were you, I would … . Let's … . Why don't you … ? You need to … . You ought to … . You should … . You'd better … .	… is worth a try. Have you thought about … ? Have you tried … ? How about … ? What about … ? In my experience, … works really well.

5 Finding the right definitions

Match the words on the left with the correct definitions on the right.

1. population	H	A	soldiers protecting the peace in an area
2. mother tongue		B	systematic study of the natural world, e.g. chemistry and physics
3. migrant worker		C	somebody who has fled his or her home country
4. refugee		D	a simple working language used for communication
5. peacekeeping troops		E	first language
6. aid worker		F	people who go to another country or another area to work there
7. lingua franca		G	someone who works for an organisation that brings food and other supplies to people in danger from wars, floods, etc.
8. science		H	all the people living in a country

It's my life
Identities – what next?

> **TIP**
> - Prime Time Transition 5: Unit 2 → S. 18
> - Prime Time 5: Unit 2 → S. 14

1 Who am I?

a) Read the self-description below and underline all the words and phrases that can be used to describe a person.

How shall I describe myself? What am I like as a person? Complicated! I'm sensitive, friendly, outgoing, popular and tolerant, though I can also be shy and self-conscious. I'd like to be friendly and tolerant all of the time. That's the kind of person I want to be, and I'm disappointed when I'm not. I'm responsible, even hard-working now and then, but on the other hand, I'm sometimes lazy too, because if you're too serious you won't be popular. I don't usually do that well at school. I'm a pretty cheerful person, especially with my friends. At home I'm more likely to be uneasy with my parents around. They expect me to get good grades all the time. It's not fair! I always worry about how I could do better. That's why I'm usually pretty stressed out at home.

But I really don't understand how I can switch so fast. I mean, how can I be cheerful one minute, worried the next, and then be frustrated and angry? Which one is the real me? I don't know who I really am! The good thing is that I don't really care what others think anyway. I don't want to care, that is. I just want to know what my close friends think.

b) Write down six words you would like to remember.

selfconscious   frustrated   tolerant
cheerful   uneasy   outgoing

2 Describing a person

a) Find eight pairs of synonyms in the word cloud.

1. angry — furious
2. quiet — silent
3. loud — noisy
4. clever — intelligent
5. horrible — terrible
6. pretty — beautiful
7. easy-going — relaxed
8. awesome — amazing

2 | It's my life • Identities – what next?

b) Use the words from page 7, task 2a, and underline the ones you would need to describe your best friend. If you find words you don't understand, use a dictionary.

c) Answer the questions below and describe your best friend. If you don't have any ideas, use the same patterns as in the example sentences.

1. What does he/she like doing? – He/She <u>likes watching</u> TV commercials.
   She likes going out with friends.

2. What does he/she do regularly? – He/She <u>calls</u> me twice a day.
   She hugs me every day.

3. What can he/she do which you can't? – He/She <u>can sing</u> much better than me.
   She is always happy and friendly.

4. What don't you like about him/her? – He/She <u>ignores</u> me sometimes.
   She ignores me sometimes.

5. What is so special about him/her? – I <u>like</u> the way he/she <u>speaks</u>.
   I love the way she always cheers me up ♡

3 Describing character

a) Turn the positive words below into negative ones by adding a suitable prefix from the blue box.

dis- • im- • in- • un-

1. <u>un</u>ambitious
2. ....flexible
3. ....friendly
4. ....happy
5. ....honest
6. ....kind
7. ....lucky
8. ....pleasant
9. ....polite
10. ....punctual
11. ....reliable
12. ....sensitive

b) Use the words from task 3a to describe the following people. Sometimes you need to use the positive form, sometimes the negative one.

1. My brother's always on time. ....punctual..........
2. She often promises to study maths with me, but half the time she forgets. ....
3. I'm prepared to work in different places and with different people everyday. ....
4. She is just never aware of what other people think or feel. ....
5. Julie wants to be head of department and then move on to a bigger company. ....
6. Since her boyfriend broke up with her, she hasn't smiled once. ....

c) Make your own sentences with the words you didn't use in the sentences above.

2 It's my life • Identities – what next?

4 Language in use: What are the qualities a good student should have?

a) You are going to read a text about personal qualities regarded necessary to be a good student. Some words are missing from the text. Choose from the list (A–L) the correct part for each gap (1–9) in the text. There are two extra words you should not use. Write your answers in the boxes provided. The first one (0) has been done for you.

It takes time to develop and sharpen the skills and qualities needed to be a … **(0)** student. You might not realise it, but you could already possess the qualities a good student needs to succeed.

Believe in yourself
Basically, it's a good start to be … **(Q1)** and to expect the best of everybody else and in every situation. It also helps to know yourself and your strengths and weaknesses well. That way, you become … **(Q2)** and can accept difficult challenges.

Time management skills
Students often lead … **(Q3)** lives. Managing your time well helps you to stay on top of your work and to succeed as a student. Limit distractions by working in a quiet area such as a library, coffee shop or home office. Call a … **(Q4)** study partner who never lets you down when you need help, and take regular breaks to help you focus.

Leadership and teamwork
As a student, you will often be paired with other students to complete a group assignment. Some of them are really … **(Q5)**, others try to avoid work. Even if you are too … **(Q6)** to fill the role, a group needs a leader who splits the workload among group members equally and fairly. If conflicts arise, be … **(Q7)** and listen to what everyone has to say before taking action.

Leading a balanced lifestyle
Leading a … **(Q8)** lifestyle is a major building block in becoming a successful student. It's crucial that you get enough sleep, on average eight to nine hours of sleep per night. To prepare for sleep, turn off all personal electronic devices, such as mobile phones and computers, before going to bed. In the morning, eat a healthy breakfast that includes protein, fruits, vegetables and grains, and be … **(Q9)** enough to do sports regularly.

(Edith Quinn, www.ehow.com; adapted and abridged)

b) What other good qualities should a student possess? Use some of the other words from this unit and write two or three more paragraphs for the article above.

3 Up and away

Up and away

> **TIP**
> • Prime Time Transition 5: Unit 3 → S. 32

1 Vocabulary revision

a) Go through the travel words below and add the words from the blue box.

> bicycle • boat • bus stop • coach • driver • ferry • first class • gate • helicopter • motorway *(BE)* • ocean liner • passenger • pilot • platform • single ticket • tourist office • tram

Tickets
bus pass, boarding pass, return ticket, business class, economy class, reservation
....
....

Roads
country road, dirt road, dead-end road, street, side street, one-way street, freeway *(AE)*, avenue
....

Rail traffic
engine, locomotive, rail carriage, dining car, sleeping car, local train, fast train, intercity train
....

Road traffic
car, taxi, bus, double decker bus, motorbike, convertible, SUV, lorry *(BE)*, truck *(AE)*, caravan, minibus, scooter
....

Places to book
ticket office, travel agent/agency, airline
....

Water traffic
sailing boat, canoe, yacht, kayak, cruiser, steamer
....

Stations
underground station *(BE)*, subway station *(AE)*, railway station
....

Places
petrol station *(BE)*, gas station *(AE)*, motorway service area *(BE)*, interstate service area *(AE)*, garage, bus terminal
....

People
conductor, train driver, bus driver, taxi driver, co-pilot, flight attendant, captain
....

Air traffic
aeroplane, jet, jumbo jet, paraglider, balloon
....

At the airport
check-in, lounge, runway, duty free shop
....

b) Make a list of the words you do not know and look them up in a dictionary.
c) Underline the words which you could use to describe your own travel experience. If you have used a tram, for example, underline "tram".

2 Vocabulary definitions

Find the right expressions for the definitions below.

1. a vehicle you can sleep in on a campsite: ....
2. where you hand over your luggage at the airport: ....
3. a boat that links two destinations on a regular basis: ....
4. a two-way ticket: ....
5. a comfortable bus, usually for long-distance travel: ....
6. the exit from the airport building to the airplane: ....

Up and away 3

3 Talking about a holiday trip

a) Match the two sets of sentence halves below and write the text down.

1. This is a great photograph …
2. In the foreground you can see …
3. The people in the picture were …
4. In the background there is …
5. The weather was …
6. The temperature was not too …
7. The picture reminds me of …
8. When I look at the picture I wish …
9. For me this picture captures this terrific holiday …

[ ] … a ferryboat taking tourists from Alcatraz, the prison island in the Bay, back to San Francisco.

[ ] … fantastic, just a slight breeze on the Bay but sunshine all the way.

[ ] … I could go back this year.

[ ] … my wonderful stay in the US last year.

[1 ✓] … of my trip to San Francisco.

[ ] … that brought America to life for me.

[ ] … the spectacular skyline of the city of San Francisco.

[ ] … visitors to the island like us.

[ ] … warm, just the right sort of weather to make a little trip.

b) Find synonyms for words referring to "travel".

holiday,

c) Find synonyms for words or phrases expressing positive quality.

great,

d) Use the text "A night to remember" on pages 34–35 in your coursebook and find synonyms for words or phrases expressing negative quality.

frightening,

3 Up and away

4 A restaurant review: Putting the record right

*Take the following review of a restaurant, which you have found on a website, and turn it into a positive description as you have had a completely different experience and you think that the criticism is unfair. In order to do this, replace negative words and phrases with positive ones. These parts of the text are printed in **bold**. Choose words and phrases from the suggestions below or find your own ones and rewrite the text.*

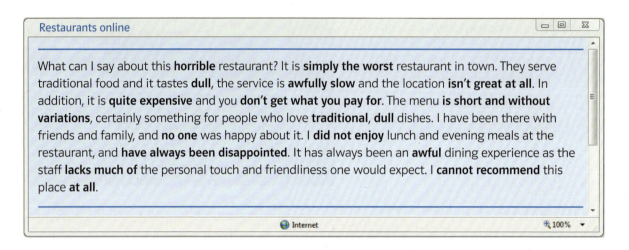

Restaurants online

What can I say about this **horrible** restaurant? It is **simply the worst** restaurant in town. They serve traditional food and it tastes **dull**, the service is **awfully slow** and the location **isn't great at all**. In addition, it is **quite expensive** and you **don't get what you pay for**. The menu **is short and without variations**, certainly something for people who love **traditional, dull** dishes. I have been there with friends and family, and **no one** was happy about it. I **did not enjoy** lunch and evening meals at the restaurant, and **have always been disappointed**. It has always been an **awful** dining experience as the staff **lacks much of** the personal touch and friendliness one would expect. I **cannot recommend** this place **at all**.

horrible: excellent – superb – great – gorgeous – charming little – wonderful – fine
simply the worst: simply the best – the most superb – the most outstanding
dull: delicious – delightful – great – excellent
awfully slow: professional – really fast – attentive – friendly – swift
isn't great at all: is gorgeous – is breath-taking – is stunning – is magnificent
quite expensive: quite reasonable – reasonably priced – cheap
don't get what you pay for: get (much) more than what you pay for – get your money's worth
is short and without variations: is large and varied – offers a large variety of dishes – will satisfy almost anyone, vegetarians included
traditional, dull: superb traditional – traditional and tasty – traditional, well-seasoned
no one: everybody – all of us – we … all
did not enjoy: really enjoyed – loved
have always been disappointed: have never been disappointed – have always got what I had expected
awful: excellent – superb – great – lovely
lacks much of: is characterised by
cannot recommend … at all: can fully recommend – can recommend … wholeheartedly

5 An emergency call

Put the following dialogue in the right order.

1 ✓	Operator:	Fire service. Can you please give me the address where the fire is?		Caroline:	No, we were the only people in the house. …
	Operator:	21 Swainstone Road, Maidstone. Thank you. Is it a house?		Caroline:	Yes, it is, a terraced house. The fire's in the upstairs bedroom!
	Operator:	Is there anyone else in the building?		Caroline:	I'm outside, with my little brother.
	Operator:	And are you outside or still in the building?		Caroline:	21 Swainstone Road in Maidstone.

Hobbies

> **TIP**
> Prime Time Transition 5: Unit 4 → S. 46

1 Interpreting graphs

Samantha carried out a survey at her school about what her schoolmates thought about the stress in their lives. She asked 92 people between the ages of 13 and 19. More than half of the interviews were done with 15- to 16-year-olds.

a) Study the two charts below and comment on them.

Teens rate their stress

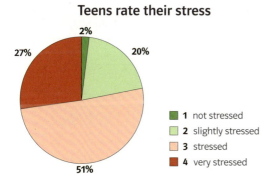

Chart 1: "How would you rate the level of stress in your life?"

How teens cope with stress

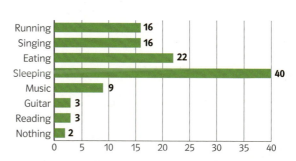

Chart 2: "What do you do to cope with the level of stress in your life?"

This ...*graph*... (1) shows that .... (2) of the people think their lives are fairly stressful. .... (3) than 50 per cent of the interviewees said their stress level was three. The second largest group are the people who have the highest stress level: .... (4) 30 per cent gave their stress level a four. There was hardly anybody who said there wasn't any stress in their lives: I'm .... (5) to see that just 2 per cent of the interviewees .... (6) their stress level was 1.

In this graph we can see that .... (7) is the number one activity for people to cope with their stress. 40 per .... (8) of the interviewees gave this answer. Eating comes in .... (9) place with 22 per cent, followed by singing with .... (10) per cent. There are .... (11) many people who go running as who sing to cope with their stress. Both activities got 16 per cent. .... (12) than 10 per cent of the interviewees listen to music in stressful times.

b) Why do you think people chose these free time activities? Write sentences.

1. Sleeping: *I think sleeping is the best way to cope with stress because it gives you new energy.*
2. Eating: ....
3. Singing: ....
4. Running: ....
5. Listening to music: ....
6. Playing the guitar: ....
7. Reading: ....
8. Doing nothing: ....

c) Collect other free time activities that might help to cope with stress.

4 Hobbies

2 Ball games

a) Write the names of the ball games below the pictures of the balls.

baseball ~~basketball~~ football golf American football table tennis tennis volleyball

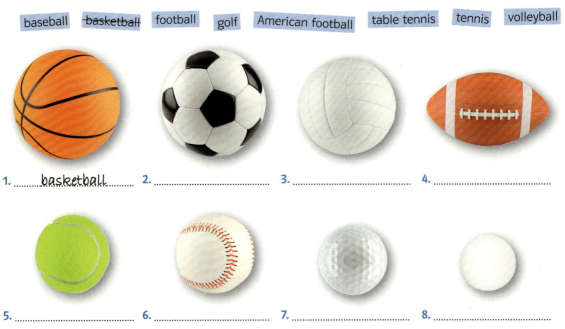

1. basketball 2. .... 3. .... 4. ....

5. .... 6. .... 7. .... 8. ....

b) What can/must/mustn't you do with the ball in these games? Write sentences according to the rules of the games.

throw it   head it   pass it   hit it   catch it   kick it

1. Basketball: In basketball you have to throw the ball and pass it to the other players. You can catch it but you mustn't kick it. You have to throw the ball into the hoop.
2. Football: ....
3. Volleyball: ....
4. Tennis: ....

3 Sports words

a) Organise these words and put them in the correct columns below.

~~circuit~~ ~~clubs~~ court crash helmet football golf net pitch pool puck racket rink skates sticks swimming trainers whistle

Sport	Place	Equipment
	circuit	clubs

b) Go on the internet and find out what sports the places and pieces of equipment above belong to.

4 Language in use: My volunteer experiences

You are going to read a text about a teenager who regularly volunteers in a nursing home. In most lines of the text there is a word that should not be there. Write that word in the space provided after each line. Some lines are correct. Indicate these lines with a tick (✓). There are three examples at the beginning.

the	0
at	00
✓	000
✓	Q1
on	Q2
✓	Q3
not	Q4
✓	Q5
did	Q6
after	Q7
✓	Q8
this	Q9
from	Q10
over	Q11
✓	Q12
because	Q13
by	Q14
✓	Q15
over	Q16
at	Q17
✓	Q18

Up until a few years ago I had never thought that **the** one of my grandparents
would be in a nursing **at** home. I had always been lucky to have them
healthy. However, this changed about a year ago when my grandfather
had a mini-stroke. From that time onward, he needed extra care if my
grandmother could not provide on. Watching my family deal with my
grandfather made me aware of the care the elderly need and has made
me realise how important it is not to volunteer at a local nursing home.
My grandfather's stroke affected his legs and his memory, which made it
difficult for him to walk. My grandfather first did used a cane, but his
legs became too weak, so after he tried a walker, but this lasted only a
month. Not only could he not walk or take care of himself, but he also
began to stay up at night and fall out of this bed.
My family started from looking into nursing homes. It took us weeks
before finally deciding over. Unfortunately he will have to stay there
until he improves, both mentally and physically.
Since summer I have volunteered at his nursing home because when I
saw how lonely some of the residents were. I volunteered by two days a
week during the summer, which I have continued. I have learned many
things about nursing homes and over the factors to consider when
choosing one, including at the residents' quality of life, the care received,
the environment surrounding them, and the payment policy.

5 Volunteering vocabulary

Complete the sentences with suitable words.

needy   soup   Corps   ~~donate~~   shelters   charity

1. Volunteer workers ....**donate**........ their time. This means that they work without receiving any money.
2. People who are homeless or poor are also referred to as the ....
3. In some cities, there are homeless .... for those who have nowhere to go.
4. Some organisations have set up .... kitchens, which provide food for free or at a very low cost.
5. People who can afford to donate money often give to .... organisations.
6. An American organisation called the Peace .... sends volunteers out to developing countries.

Fifteen minutes of fame
Media-mad

TIP
- Prime Time Transition 5: Unit 5 → S. 58
- Prime Time 5: Unit 4 → S. 44

1 On TV

a) Here are the evening programmes of four British TV channels. Find examples of:

a documentary   a quiz show   a game show
a drama series   a current affairs programme

BBC 1	BBC 2	ITV 1	Channel 4
17:15 Pointless (Quiz show) Pairs of contestants try to score the fewest points possible	**17:15** Antiques Roadshow (Documentary) M. Aspel and his team of experts search for antique treasures	**17:00** The Chase (Quiz show) Four contestants play against a quiz genius called the chaser	**17:00** Come Dine with Me (Game show) Four amateur chefs in Swansea compete to win the £1,000 prize
18:00 BBC News **18:30** BBC London News	**18:00** Eggheads (Quiz Show) Quiz in which the winners of famous game shows work as a team **18:30** Country Show Cook Off (Documentary) The chefs today set up their kitchen to prepare open fruit pies	**18:00** ITV News London **18:30** ITV News and Weather	**18:00** The Simpsons (Cartoon) The family goes away to Marge's favourite childhood holiday destination **18:30** Hollyoaks (Drama) The circumstances of Holly's sudden disappearance remain a mystery
19:00 The One Show (Magazine) Live magazine show featuring celebrity chat and stories of interest **19:30** EastEnders (Soap) Ava and Dexter catch up with Liam, finding him bloodied after a gang fight	**19:00** Great British Menu (Game show) The finalists prepare their desserts and author and comedian Charlie Higson helps judge them	**19:00** Emmerdale (Drama) When Robbie starts smashing bottles, the situation takes a twist **19:30** Breadline Britain: Tonight (Documentary) Many "working poor" families, despite having a job, live in shocking conditions	**19:00** Channel 4 News **19:55** Easter Eggs Live (Documentary) Follow the hatchings of a variety of creatures. Today: Crocodiles
20:00 MasterChef (Game show) Another group of contestants takes a cooking test but without a recipe	**20:00** James May's Man Lab (Documentary) James May continues to help modern men relearn vital skills	**20:00** Emmerdale (Drama) Gemma takes revenge on Belle as Charity agrees to hire Rachel as a cleaner **20:30** The Martin Lewis Money Show (Documentary) The financial guru offers advice on finding hidden payments	**20:00** Secret Eaters (Documentary) Anna Richardson puts more overweight households under 24-hour surveillance

 b) Go on the internet and find out more about a show of your choice.

Fifteen minutes of fame • Media-mad | **5**

2 TV vocabulary

a) Complete the sentences with suitable expressions. There are three extra words you should not use.

soap opera · actor · quiz show · host · remote control · ~~coverage~~ · prime time · on air · breaking · anchors · channel · forecast · rerun · sitcom

1. Turn on the telly! There is live ......**coverage**...... of the football match between ManU and Chelsea.
2. Those were today's headlines. And now it's Amy Mallatratt with the weather ....
3. Pass me the .... I'd like to switch to another ....
4. A .... is a kind of TV drama which is based on the relationships between people and usually has a very simple plot.
5. There's just some .... news coming in that an earthquake has affected large parts of Japan.
6. *The Weakest Link* is a very popular .... , broadcast daily on BBC television.
7. The time of day when most people are watching TV is known as ....
8. Welcome to this live TV debate on the upcoming elections. Our .... is as usual Bill Morton, and his guests today are the leaders of the two opposing parties.
9. A .... is a repeat broadcast of a show.
10. The people who read the news on TV are called news ....

b) Write your own sentences with the three words you didn't use in the task.

3 In the movies

a) Match the words on the left with the explanations on the right.

1. to rave about something	F	A	actor who may replace the main actor
2. slow motion		B	highly popular film
3. blockbuster		C	background characters who don't have a speaking part
4. understudy		D	film made with computer graphics
5. movie buff		E	film running slower than at normal speed
6. credits		F	to praise
7. props		G	someone who knows a lot about films
8. extras		H	names that appear at the end of the film
9. voice-over		I	film translated into another language using voice-overs
10. digitally animated film		J	objects used in a film scene
11. dubbed film		K	translation using words along the bottom of the screen
12. subtitles		L	voice of the narrator

b) Write sentences into your notebook, using the words you defined in task 3a.

5 Fifteen minutes of fame • Media-mad

4 Language in use: Teen television addiction

You are going to read a text about television addiction among teenagers. Some words are missing from the text. Use the words in brackets to complete each gap (1–11) in the text. Write your answers in the spaces provided at the end of the text. The first one (0) has been done for you.

Television shows such as *90210*, *The Secret Life of the American Teenager* and *Pretty Little Liars* have created addiction among teenagers. They are … **(0 design)** to make teens watch a certain show for weeks on end, whether it is for one or eight seasons. "I just love *Pretty Little Liars*, and I have watched it since day one," student Leah Tepera said. "It is so … **(Q1 addiction)** because every episode has a huge cliffhanger at the end. You just have to watch the next episode to find out what happens next."

The … **(Q2 produce)** and directors of the show have a way of making the plot very realistic. The girls in the series have to go through the same things as regular teens, such as boyfriends and … **(Q3 problem)** families. This makes shows like this especially … **(Q4 attraction)** to teenage girls. "The problem with teen TV addiction is that kids are not interacting with other people and are not getting out there and have a … **(Q5 reality)** relationship with their friends and family," Spanish teacher Judy Garret said.

Yet not all TV shows are a success from beginning to end. Some series have an original and … **(Q6 promise)** start, but after a few seasons are regarded by students as boring and repetitive. However, some teens will still continue to watch the show out of … **(Q7 curious)** about what happens to the characters. In the end, they will have used their time watching a show for so long that has turned out to be boring.

One example for this phenomenon is *The Secret Life of the American Teenager*. When this show was first aired, it contained an original plot about the … **(Q8 grow)** number of pregnant teenagers. With the show reaching its … **(Q9 five)** season this March, it now focuses on the struggle of being a teen rushed into parenthood. "I used to watch *The Secret Life of the American Teenager* back in middle school, but I … **(Q10 final)** stopped when almost every girl in the school got pregnant," junior Bailey Farrell said. "The show got so boring I had to quit. It was hard to stop at first but new shows like *Pretty Little Liars* came out which were ten times more interesting."

Like in every addiction, there are always some major consequences. For some, television takes up more than five hours of their time per week. Important things like homework and grades are put on hold when students spend hours watching their … **(Q11 favour)** shows.

0	designed ✔	Q6	....
Q1	....	Q7	....
Q2	....	Q8	....
Q3	....	Q9	....
Q4	....	Q10	....
Q5	....	Q11	....

5 Agree to disagree

Complete the following phrases with suitable words to express an opinion.

A: I'm ..worried.. **(1)** about the effect of violence and swearing in many of today's TV programmes.

B: I'm .... **(2)** I don't agree with you. I don't .... **(3)** that has much effect on how people behave and talk themselves. In my .... **(4)**, it's families and friends that people get their values from.

A: I'm afraid I see it .... **(5)**. I'm .... **(6)** that what people see on their screens does have some influence.

Music

1 Vocabulary revision: Music production

> **TIP**
> - Prime Time Transition 5: Unit 6 → S. 72
> - Prime Time 5: Unit 8 → S. 98

Study the picture and then complete the table below. If you are short of ideas, go back to the texts in your coursebook.

Producing your own music	Equipment needed	Songs
edit music	multi-track audio recorder	tune

6 Music

2 Language in use: The history of sound recording

You are going to read a text about the history of sound recording. Some words are missing from the text. Choose from the list (A–L) the correct part for each gap (1–9) in the text. There are two extra words you should not use. Write your answers in the boxes provided. The first one (0) has been done for you.

In the late 19th century Thomas Alva Edison invented the first sound-… **(0)** machine, which he called the phonograph. This was a machine that used wax cylinders to … **(Q1)** musical data. Emile Berliner introduced flat discs to record sounds as early as 1889. These … **(Q2)** were easier to handle and became the fore-runners of … **(Q3)** discs, which came into fashion in the 20th century. All these processes were analogue, which means that the sound waves were recorded by changing the surface of the … **(Q4)** or disc, which was used for the process. In the 1920s electromagnetic recordings were first introduced and changed the whole industry. Since then the … **(Q5)** has increased steadily. The most modern way to record sound is … **(Q6)** recording. The sound waves that hit the … **(Q7)** are transformed into … **(Q8)** signals, which can be stored as computer data on a storage … **(Q9)** like a CD, a hard disk or a flash drive (e.g. a mobile phone).

A	cylinder	F	microphone	K	tape
B	digital	G	recording	L	vinyl
C	discs	H	singer		
D	electromagnetic	I	sound quality		
E	medium	J	store		

0: G ✓

Q1, Q2, Q3, Q4, Q5, Q6, Q7, Q8, Q9

3 Discussing a song

Fill the gaps with suitable adjectives.

> aggressive • exciting • fast • loud • melodious • modern • monotonous • simple • slow • ~~soft~~

1. The singer's voice is very gentle, but for me it is too ....**soft**........ .
2. No one else has ever played such a song before – it is really ....
3. The lyrics are always the same – it is such a .... song.
4. The tune sounds really good because the song is so ....
5. The tune is played at a high speed, it is quite ....

20

6. You can sing the song easily because the lyrics and the tune are very ....

7. For me this song is boring, just a bit too ....

8. I prefer something more ....

9. But the rhythm should not be too fast. That would sound too ....

10. I can't stand this number when they play live because it is so ....

4 File sharing: Is it worth the trouble?

a) What are your views on file sharing? Tick (✓) the sentences that best reflect your opinion.

File sharing
- ☐ is unfair, because people get songs without paying for them.
- ☐ is great because you can get songs very cheaply.
- ☐ is a good opportunity to collect music on your hard disk.
- ☐ is much better than stealing CDs from a shop.
- ☐ is nothing more than theft, you steal other people's property.
- ☐ means a new way of distributing music.
- ☐ leads to a lot of problems for the music industry.
- ☐ causes problems for people who want to sell their music.
- ☐ should be banned because it is illegal.
- ☐ is not really a crime for me.
- ☐ should be made illegal to protect the rights of the song writers and artists.
- ☐ should not be supported by anybody.
- ☐ is regarded to be a minor offence, not worth talking about.
- ☐ is immensely popular, especially among young internet users.
- ☐ is something we all pay for because legal downloads become more expensive.
- ☐ could help unknown artists to become famous.
- ☐ could make it possible for smaller bands to publish their music widely and at very low cost.

b) Rewrite the statements you have ticked in a logical order. If possible, connect them with linking words. Use words like:

and • but • in addition • moreover • however • because

7 Jobs

Jobs

> **TIP**
> • Prime Time Transition 5: Unit 7 → S. 86
> • Prime Time 5: Unit 9 → S. 112

1 Different jobs for different people

a) Complete each of the definitions with one of the jobs. Use a dictionary to look up the jobs you don't know.

accountant ~~architect~~ bricklayer ~~carpenter~~ dentist ~~doctor~~ electrician ~~engineer~~ ~~firefighter~~ ~~lawyer~~ mechanic nurse ~~plumber~~ police officer sales manager soldier ~~stockbroker~~ ~~university lecturer~~ ~~vet~~

1. A _university lecturer_ teaches at university.
2. An _architect_ designs buildings.
3. A _lawyer_ represents people with legal problems.
4. An _engineer_ plans the construction of roads, bridges or machines.
5. A _doctor_ cares for sick people and provides medical assistance.
6. A _stockbroker_ buys and sells stocks and shares.
7. A _vet_ treats sick or injured animals.
8. A _carpenter_ builds and repairs wooden things, especially the wooden parts of buildings or ships.
9. A _plumber_ installs, repairs or works with pipes and water supplies.
10. A _firefighter_ extinguishes fires and rescues people and animals.

b) Write your own definitions for the jobs you didn't use above.

c) Write down one job from the list above that would be hard for these people to do. Explain why you chose these jobs.

1. Someone who didn't go to university: _lawyer_
2. Someone who understands nothing about cars: _mechanic_
3. Someone who doesn't want to work in the evening or at weekends: _nurse_
4. Someone who can't see very well: _dentist_
5. Someone who can't see blood: _doctor_
6. Someone who isn't physically fit: _bricklayer_
7. Someone who is afraid of dogs: _vet_
8. Someone who is terrible at numbers and maths: _university lecturer_
9. Someone who is afraid of heights: _firefighter_
10. Someone who is a pacifist: _soldier_

2 Moving up the career ladder

a) Match the words on the left with the correct definitions on the right.

#	Word	Answer	Letter	Definition
1.	abroad	D	A	work in a different kind of job
2.	to apply for	F	B	person employed for wages or salary
3.	career change	A	C	future possibilities in the job
4.	to dismiss	G	D	in another country
5.	employee	B	E	more money every month
6.	in-house training	I	F	write an official request
7.	part-time job	J	G	tell somebody to leave
8.	pay rise	E	H	a person who is learning the skills of a particular job
9.	to promote	M	I	courses offered by a company for its employees
10.	prospects	C	J	working only part of the day or week
11.	to resign	N	K	stop working completely
12.	to retire	K	L	without a job
13.	trainee	H	M	give a higher position with more money and responsibility
14.	unemployed	L	N	tell the company that you are leaving your job

b) You are going to read a text about Sheera's career. Some words are missing from the text. Choose from the list (A–L) the correct part for each gap (1–9) in the text. There are two extra words you should not use. Write your answers in the boxes provided. The first one (0) has been done for you.

When Sheera took her A-levels, she … (0) a job in various companies in her home town. One company gave her a job as a trainee. Though she didn't earn much in that position, she was happy because the company offered her … (Q1) and she went on a number of training courses. Sheera worked hard and her prospects looked good. The manager was pleased with her progress and soon offered her a … (Q2). After two years she was promoted and after four years she was in charge of a department with three … (Q3) under her.

By the time Sheera turned 35, she decided she wanted a new challenge and a … (Q4). She wanted to get some experience … (Q5), preferably in the United States or in South Africa. So Sheera resigned and started looking for another job. After a few weeks she got a job with an international company which involved a lot of foreign travel. At the beginning, Sheera was very excited about travelling to so many different places, but after six months she started to dislike living in hotels. She didn't do well in her job either. After a year the company … (Q6) her.

Life got hard for Sheera. She was … (Q7) for a year until she got a … (Q8) in a pub for four evenings per week. Sheera loved her new job. She enjoyed taking care of the patrons and three years later she took over the pub. After one and a half years she opened a second pub, and after fifteen years she had a chain of eight pubs all over Britain. Last year, Sheera … (Q9) at the age of 62.

A	abroad	F	employees	K	unemployed	0	B	Q5	A
B	applied for	G	in-house training	L	working hours	Q1	G	Q6	E
C	career change	H	part-time job			Q2	I	Q7	K
D	customer service	I	pay rise			Q3	F	Q8	H
E	dismissed	J	retired			Q4	C	Q9	J

7 Jobs

3 Crossword puzzle

a) Fill the jobs described below into the crossword puzzle.

Across
Find somebody who …
1. … catches fish.
2. … digs for coal in the ground.
7. … paints pictures.
8. … creates computer games.
9. … assists a doctor.
10. … fixes teeth.
13. … travels to outer space.
15. … treats sick animals.
18. … builds houses (two words).
20. … prepares food.
22. … fights in wars.
23. … tells us the news.
24. … does sports professionally.

Down
Find somebody who …
1. … puts out fires.
2. … plays an instrument.
3. … treats sick people.
4. … catches criminals (two words).
5. … fixes toilets.
6. … does research.
11. … cleans buildings.
12. … acts in movies.
14. … drives a truck (two words).
16. … repairs cars.
17. … sings songs.
19. … flies planes.
21. … serves food.

b) Some jobs are only included in the male form. Find the correct terms for the female forms and write them down.

actor → actress
waiter → waitress

Crime and suspense

1 Word search: Crime

a) *Find as many words as you can that have something to do with crime. You'll find the words reading from left to right (→), from right to left (←), from top to bottom (↓) and from bottom to top (↑).*

T	F	E	H	T	G	Z	K	J	G	Z	N
Y	S	K	I	D	N	A	P	P	I	N	G
S	H	O	P	L	I	F	T	I	N	G	A
E	G	J	C	H	L	N	U	B	N	R	R
C	M	S	I	N	A	G	I	L	O	O	H
N	B	R	I	B	E	R	Y	A	S	B	K
E	M	I	R	C	D	N	H	C	R	B	C
F	G	N	I	G	G	U	M	K	A	E	A
F	R	E	D	R	U	M	F	M	E	R	T
O	A	B	B	U	R	G	L	A	R	Y	T
W	P	V	A	N	D	A	L	I	S	M	A
C	E	A	S	M	U	G	G	L	E	V	Z

b) *Now fill in the definitions with the words from task 1a.*

1. When you steal something: ← T _ _ _ _
2. Taking something by threatening people: ↓ R _ _ _ _ _ _
3. Destroying things without a good reason: → V _ _ _ _ _ _ _ _
4. Selling illegal substances: ↑ D _ _ _ - _ _ _ _ _ _ _ _
5. Taking something from a shop without paying: → S _ _ _ _ _ _ _ _ _ _
6. Breaking into a house: → B _ _ _ _ _ _ _
7. Breaking the law: ↑ O _ _ _ _ _ _
8. Demanding money for releasing a person: ↓ B _ _ _ _ _ _
9. Taking something across the border illegally: → S _ _ _ _ _ _ _
10. Killing somebody with intent: ← M _ _ _ _ _ _
11. When football fans behave badly: ← H _ _ _ _ _ _ _ _ _ _
12. Setting fire to a building: ↑ A _ _ _ _
13. Giving somebody money for an illegal favour: → B _ _ _ _ _ _
14. A sexual attack on a person: ↓ R _ _ _
15. Abducting a person: → K _ _ _ _ _ _ _ _
16. Violence against people (e.g. beating): ↑ A _ _ _ _ _ _
17. A general expression for what criminals do: ← C _ _ _ _ _
18. Robbery (with a knife): ← M _ _ _ _ _ _

> **TIP**
> Prime Time Transition 5: Unit 8 → S. 100

8 | Crime and suspense

2 Language in use: Alfred Hitchcock – The Master of Suspense

You are going to read a text about Alfred Hitchcock, the Master of Suspense. Some words are missing from the text. Choose from the list (A–N) the correct part for each gap (1–11) in the text. There are two extra words you should not use. Write your answers in the boxes provided. The first one (0) has been done for you.

The British filmmaker and … **(0)** Alfred Hitchcock (1899–1980) was one of the most important and most famous directors of … **(Q1)** of his time. Many of his movies are psychological … **(Q2)**. When you watch one of his films you can never be sure how the story will end. He also tried to fool his … **(Q3)** by adding mysteries to the stories so that the … **(Q4)** were confused about the outcome of the plot. Keeping important information from the audience is a typical … **(Q5)** of his films. This is the reason why he was also called the "Master of Suspense". But it was not just his … **(Q6)** telling stories that made him so important. In addition to that he … **(Q7)** a lot of different ways how to use the camera in order to make his movies even more impressive.

But he was also a man with a … **(Q8)** of humour. In each of his films he also plays a small part. Sometimes he just walks through the background of a scene or sometimes you may only see the … **(Q9)** of his round figure with a cigar in his mouth.

He started his career in Great Britain, but in 1939 he moved to Hollywood to work for the American … **(Q10)**. Altogether he directed more than fifty feature films. Today he is … **(Q11)** as the greatest British filmmaker of all times.

A	audience	G̶	producer	M	viewers	0	G ✓	Q6	
B	feature	H	publication	N	way of	Q1		Q7	
C	good sense	I	regarded			Q2		Q8	
D	invented	J	shadow			Q3		Q9	
E	masterpieces	K	shot			Q4		Q10	
F	movie industry	L	thrillers			Q5		Q11	

3 Finding definitions: Thrillers

Use the words in the blue box to fill in the right expressions for the definitions provided on page 27.

> audience • background • career • ~~director~~ • end • feature film • film industry •
> masterpiece • mystery • part • plot • producer •
> scene • suspense • thriller • viewer

Crime and suspense | **8**

1. a person in charge of filmmaking: *director*
2. the people watching a movie or a play: ....
3. a short part of a movie: ....
4. the person who is in charge of a film's production: ....
5. a full-length film for entertainment: ....
6. a person watching a movie in a cinema: ....
7. a movie about a crime story: ....
8. the final part of a movie: ....
9. the opposite of foreground: ....
10. all the filmmakers and film companies together: ....
11. a very good film: ....
12. something you cannot explain: ....
13. what an actor or an actress plays in a movie: ....
14. a state of feeling excited about the unknown ending of a movie: ....
15. the main events of the story, a movie or a play: ....
16. your successful professional life: ....

4 Language in use: A crime story by Patricia Highsmith

You are going to read a text about a crime story by Patricia Highsmith. In most lines of the text there is a word that should not be there. Write that word in the space provided after each line. Some lines are correct. Indicate these lines with a tick (✓). There are three examples at the beginning.

Text	Answer	#
In this text Particia Highsmith tells the story of woman who has	✓	0
lost interest in **to** her husband. So she decides to kill him.	to	00
But she does not want to do this openly. As she knows that her	✓	000
husband has heart attack problems she starts cooking very rich		Q1
meals for him – everything her husband should not eat.		Q2
Gradually her husband gets more and more health problems.		Q3
He is short of breath, his lonely heart starts aching. One day his		Q4
wife pretends that she is not well and asks her husband to carry		Q5
her out upstairs. This turns out to be too much for him.		Q6
He puts her in her bed and then lately he falls on his bed and starts		Q7
breathing heavily strong. As there is nothing wrong with his wife,		Q8
she could call for help. Instead she stays with him, but does		Q9
not help him and so he dies away. All the people in her road		Q10
come and tell to her how sorry they are for her that her husband		Q11
has died. And she pretends to be an honourable widow.		Q12
On the one hand this story shows that Patricia Highsmith could		Q13
write very interesting but also very exciting stories. On the very		Q14
other hand this story is also a good working example of her		Q15
rather dark sense of her humour. Altogether this text is		Q16
entertaining and well worth reading.		Q17

Australia

1 Language in use: The Great Barrier Reef

You are going to read a text about the Great Barrier Reef in Australia. Some words are missing from the text. Choose the correct answer (A, B, C or D) for each gap (1–10) in the text. Write your answers in the boxes provided. The first one (0) has been done for you.

> **TIP**
> • Prime Time Transition 5: Unit 9 → S. 116
> • Prime Time 5: Unit 3 → S. 30

The Great Barrier Reef is the … **(0)** coral reef in the world. It … **(Q1)** off the east coast of Australia. Altogether it is about 2,600 kilometres long and … **(Q2)** about 2,900 reefs and about 900 islands. But even though it seems so big and … **(Q3)** many experts believe that it will not survive the next forty years. A reef consists of corals which are … **(Q4)** living in the sea. Their skeletons form the structure of the reef. If these corals are threatened by climate change or by … **(Q5)** through chemicals, they will die. When the water temperature rises above 28 °C the corals cannot survive. If that happens, other animals that live in the reef will also … **(Q6)**. Scientists even say that a lot of damage has already been done because more than 50 per cent of the reef's coral cover has been lost since 1985. If this goes on, the very … **(Q7)** ecosystem of the reef will soon be gone.

That is the reason why the Australian Government makes great … **(Q8)** to protect the natural structure and the wildlife in the reefs. Part of the areas has been declared a wildlife park which makes it possible to … **(Q9)** tourism and also fishing.

… **(Q10)** its biological function the Great Barrier Reef also plays an important role in the culture of the Aboriginal Australians and Torres Strait Islanders.

0	A	widest	B	greatest	¢	largest	D	broadest
Q1	A	is seated	B	is situated	C	sitting	D	situates
Q2	A	competes	B	complements	C	consists of	D	contains
Q3	A	indestructible	B	undefended	C	indefensible	D	inconsistent
Q4	A	organists	B	organisers	C	organs	D	organisms
Q5	A	pollen	B	pollution	C	polling	D	pollutants
Q6	A	despair	B	dissolve	C	disengage	D	disappear
Q7	A	diverse	B	different	C	various	D	varied
Q8	A	effects	B	efforts	C	affects	D	affords
Q9	A	reduce	B	replace	C	resource	D	retain
Q10	A	Adding to	B	Added to	C	Additionally	D	In addition to

0	Q1	Q2	Q3	Q4	Q5	Q6	Q7	Q8	Q9	Q10
C ✓										

2 Vocabulary revision: Angela

Match the words and phrases with expressions of the same meaning.

1. recently	G	A	ready to give freely
2. politically active		B	you wish that something hadn't happened
3. rally		C	She could not be stopped.
4. mood		D	a place where you can ask for things you don't know
5. to be upset		E	a piece of clothing
6. overalls		F	demonstration
7. information booth		G	lately
8. to regret		H	to hide inside yourself, not letting others know
9. to draw a crowd		I	taking part in political activities
10. generous		J	to be unhappy, disappointed
11. There was no holding back.		K	to attract the attention of people
12. to bottle up		L	the way you feel

3 Linking sentences with *who* or *which/that*

*Combine two sentences each with the suitable relative pronoun (**who** or **which/that**).*

1. Gracey is a part-Aboriginal **girl**. – **She** comes from a poor background.

   ....

2. At university Gracey has met a new set of Aboriginal **friends**. – **They** are politically active.

   ....

3. She likes going shopping with her friend **Angela**. – **She** is white and comes from a rich background.

   ....

4. One day they went together to **a jewellery store**. – **This store** was in a big shopping mall.

   ....

5. Angela did not notice Gracey's **bad mood**. – **Her mood** had been building up for a long time.

   ....

6. In front of a shop Gracey got in trouble because she had an argument with **the shop manager**. – **The shop manager** told Gracey to move away from the shop entrance.

   ....
   ....

9 | Australia

4 Linking sentences with *and*, *but* or *because*

Combine the two sentences with **and**, **but** *or* **because**.

1. Gracey is angry. – She thinks that Angela does not understand her.
   ....
   ....

2. Angela wants to help Gracey. – Gracey starts shouting at her.
   ....
   ....

3. Gracey has a fierce argument with Angela. – Then she leaves.
   ....
   ....

5 Word formation: Prefixes

a) Form as many new words as you can and write them down.

Prefixes: dis-, out-, mis-, over-, un-, re-

Suffixes/stems: -changed, -rated, -dated, -built, -spelled, -led, -laid, -charge, -play, -born

....

b) Now match the words you have formed with the explanations below.

1. old, not modern any more: ....
2. the same as before: ....
3. reconstructed: ....
4. show: ....
5. have a better opinion of sth./sb. than is deserved: ....
6. restore the electric power of a battery: ....
7. not born yet: ....
8. you cannot find it: ....
9. without a date: ....
10. not written correctly: ....
11. deceived, tricked: ....

Books

1 Positive, negative or both?

The adjectives below can be used to describe books and literature. Some of them have a positive meaning, some have a negative meaning, some can be used either way. Put them into the appropriate boxes.

amazing · astonishing · authentic · award-winning · believable · bestselling · boring · clever · disturbing · exciting · extraordinary · far-fetched · fascinating · fast-paced · frightening · funny · heart-breaking · hilarious · honest · impressive · incredible · inspirational · magical · memorable · monumental · moving · original · predictable · realistic · refreshing · revealing · shocking · slow-moving · spectacular · stereotypical · thought-provoking · thrilling · touching · unique · weak · well-written

Positive	Negative	Both
amazing, astonishing, authentic, award-winning, believable, bestselling, clever, extraordinary, fascinating, funny, hilarious, honest, impressive, incredible, magical, memorable, moving, original, refreshing, thrilling, touching, unique, spectacular	boring, disturbing, far-fetched, frightening, predictable, shocking, weak, stereotypical	exciting, fast-paced, heart-breaking, monumental, revealing, realistic, slow-moving, thought-provoking

TIP
- Prime Time Transition 5: Unit 10 → S. 132
- Prime Time 5: Unit 10 → S. 126

2 Sentence builder

Take one word/sentence fragment from each section and make a sentence with them. Write the sentences down on page 32. You can include your own ideas.

A	B	C
award-winning	1. ~~author~~	has been in business for more than thirty years
fast-paced	2. blurb	reveals the positive and the negative sides of the book
informative	3. final chapter	the hero finally married his love
heart-breaking	4. characters	is described in great detail
hilarious	5. cover	make this book memorable and thought-provoking
honest	6. ending	makes this book a real page-turner
original	7. introduction	is necessary to understand the rather complicated plot
realistic	8. plot	kept me sleepless for days
spectacular	9. publishing house	made me laugh out loud many times
~~talented~~	10. review	~~published the new part of the vampire hit series~~
thrilling	11. setting	made me really interested in the book
well-written	12. story	usually grabs everybody's attention

1. The talented author recently published the new part of the vampire hit series The last bite.
2. The well-written blurb made me really interest in the book
3. In the heart breaking final chapter the hero finally married
4. The realistic characters make this book memorable.
5. The original cover showing a picture of Picasso grabs attention
6. The fast-paced ending was exciting so it kept me sleepless
7. The informative introduction is necessary to the book
8. The thrilling plot makes this book a real page-turner
9. The award-winning publishing house has been in business long
10. The honest review reveals the positive side of the book
11. The setting is discribed in great detail
12. The story made me laugh many times

3 Word search: Books

a) Find the following expressions in the grid below. Make sure to look in all possible directions (→, ←, ↓, ↑, ↘, ↖, ↙, ↗).

adventure biography diary dictionary drama fable fantasy handbook

horror mystery novel poem romance speech thriller

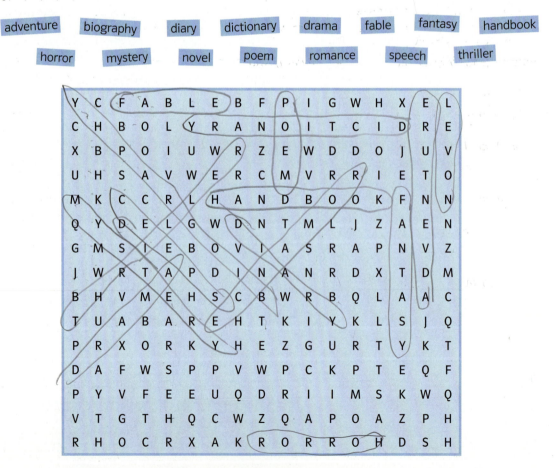

b) Use the words from task 3a on page 32 in the sentences below. Words you don't need to use are "adventure", "drama", "novel" and "romance".

1. Have you read Lady Gaga's ….. *biography* …..? I'm really impressed by her life.
2. Recently, I've started writing ….. *poems* …... My girlfriend likes it when I write one for her.
3. I don't like reading ….. *thrillers* …... I always get frightened that I might be chased by a criminal one day too.
4. Have you seen my ….. *dictionary* ….. ? The internet is down and I need to check a word!
5. Do you mean the ….. *fable* ….. with the rabbit and the hedgehog? That's a funny one!
6. I wouldn't have expected Martin Luther King's ….. *speeches* ….. to be as fascinating to read as to listen to.
7. What would I do without the gardening ….. *handbook* ….. ? My garden would be such a mess!
8. At school we're reading the ….. *diary* ….. of Anne Frank at the moment.
9. ….. *horror* ….. stories don't frighten me. I don't believe in monsters and ghosts!
10. My favourite books are ….. *fantasy* ….. novels with lots of vampires, elves and leprechauns.

4 Language in use: Book review of *Twilight* by Stephenie Meyer

You are going to read a book review. Some words are missing from the text. Use the words in brackets to complete each gap (1–10) in the text. Write your answers in the spaces provided at the end of the text. The first one (0) has been done for you.

I really never … (**0 love**) vampires until *Twilight* came out. I didn't know it was … (**Q1 possibility**), but Stephenie Meyer changed the … (**Q2 stereotype**) blood-sucking vampire into a … (**Q3 beauty**) god-like creature. In *Twilight*, an average high school girl, Bella Swan, falls in love with one of the most gorgeous boys at her new school, Edward, who happens to be a vampire. What does one call a stunning, … (**Q4 mystery**) vampire and his good-looking, … (**Q5 fascination**) vampire family? "The Cullens", that's right!

The author's style and characters will glue your hands to the book and your eyes to the page. In no time, the book is over. But don't worry – there are three sequels: *New Moon*, *Eclipse* and *Breaking Dawn*. *Twilight* is … (**Q6 write**) from Bella's point of view. It feels as though a movie is playing in your head. If you don't feel that way, have no fear, the real movies … (**Q7 actual**) have already come out.

Twilight is such a magnificent book that it was a New York Times bestseller. Who would have thought that the idea for such a … (**Q8 wonder**) book could come from a dream the author had? Meyer's style of writing will have you wanting to believe that there are gorgeous vampires roaming our world. You'll hope there will be Edwards for all of the girls who have fallen in love with this fictional … (**Q9 characteristic**). Since Bella and Edward's love is forbidden, it only makes it better. After all, forbidden fruit tastes the … (**Q10 sweet**).

0	loved ✓
Q1	possible
Q2	stereotypical
Q3	beautiful
Q4	mysterious
Q5	fascinating
Q6	written
Q7	actually
Q8	wonderful
Q9	character
Q10	sweetest

11 | Politics

Politics

> **TIP**
> • Prime Time 5: Unit 5 → S. 60

1 Word search: Politics

a) Find as many words as you can that have something to do with politics in the UK and in America. There are six possible directions in which you'll find them (→, ←, ↓, ↑, ↙, ↗).

G	E	M	I	R	P	R	M	P	T	E
N	R	J	N	G	E	A	R	N	M	T
I	U	Q	C	B	J	E	E	S	M	A
L	L	W	M	O	S	M	S	N	C	D
L	E	E	R	I	N	S	E	O	O	I
O	M	I	D	R	E	T	P	I	M	D
P	T	E	E	R	A	N	A	T	M	N
Y	N	V	G	N	G	E	R	C	O	A
T	O	N	E	Z	B	E	T	E	N	C
G	O	S	U	P	Q	U	Y	L	S	Z
C	V	O	T	E	R	Q	Q	E	Q	G

b) Now fill in the definitions with the words from task 1a.

1. A person who wants to be elected: ↑ C **A N D I D A T E**
2. House of … (part of the houses of Parliament): ↓ C **O M M O N S**
3. Senate + House of Representatives = … : ↗ C **O N G R E S S**
4. When people vote: ↑ E **L E C T I O N S**
5. The group of people who rule a country: ↗ G **O V E R N M E N T**
6. More than half of the votes: ↙ M **A J O R I T Y**
7. If you are elected you become a … of Parliament: ↗ M **E M B E R**
8. A group of people with the same political views: ↓ P **A R T Y**
9. What people do when they vote: ↑ P **O L L I N G**
10. The American head of state: ↙ P **R E S I D E N T**
11. … Minister (head of government in the UK): ← P **R I M E**
12. Head of state of the UK: ↑ Q **U E E N**
13. What the government does: ↓ R **U L E**
14. One house of the Congress: ↗ S **E N A T E**
15. Person who casts his or her vote in elections: → V **O T E R**

34

Politics

2 Language in use: The American Revolution

You are going to read a text about the American Revolution. Some words are missing from the text. Choose from the list (A–N) the correct part for each gap (1–11) in the text. There are two extra words you should not use. Write your answers in the boxes provided. The first one (0) has been done for you.

Before the United States of America were … **(0)**, British settlers set up colonies in America. Other nations like France also tried to establish … **(Q1)** in North America. However, in the course of the 18th century Britain … **(Q2)** of large areas on the East Coast. They formed thirteen colonies which served as … **(Q3)** of the British Crown.

As the wars in Europe cost enormous amounts of money, Britain tried to … **(Q4)** as many taxes and customs duties from the colonies as possible. This … **(Q5)** a lot of tensions between the colonies and their home country, especially as the settlers in the colonies did not have the … **(Q6)** for the British Parliament. Their slogan "No taxation without representation" became a powerful battle cry. The British sent more and more troops to America to … **(Q7)** with the protests, and soon the settlers in the colonies were fighting against the British soldiers – a … **(Q8)** broke out in 1775. A year later, on 4 July 1776, the colonies declared their … **(Q9)**. This is the reason why this day is a national holiday in the United States. From then on the leaders of the United States … **(Q10)** a democratic system based on the American Constitution, which is still in place today. For many European countries the American Revolution became the model for their own efforts to … **(Q11)** democracy.

A	collect	G	introduce	M	take in	0	D ✓	Q6	K
B	come to terms	H	led to	N	territories	Q1	L	Q7	B
C	formed	I	outposts			Q2	E	Q8	J
D	founded	J	revolution			Q3	I	Q9	F
E	gained control	K	right to vote			Q4	A	Q10	C
F	independence	L	settlements			Q5	H	Q11	G

3 Research: The fathers of the American Revolution

Go on the internet. Find two important leaders of the United States in 1776 and write their names into the grid.

1.	G	O	E	R	G	E		W	A	S	H	I	N	G	T	O	N
2.	T	H	O	M	A	S		J	E	F	F	E	R	S	O	N	

12 | Strange realities

Strange realities

TIP
• Prime Time 5: Unit 6 → S. 74

1 Language in use: A strange story

You are going to read a strange story. Some words are missing from the text. Use the words in brackets to complete each gap (1–11) in the text. Write your answers in the spaces provided at the end of the text. The first one (0) has been done for you.

In a small American town there once lived an honest family by the name of Smothers. The family consisted of John Smothers, an … **(0 art)**, his wife and their little five-year-old daughter Anne.

One night after dinner little Anne was seized with a severe colic, and John Smothers hurried downtown to get some medicine. "Be … **(Q1 care)**, my dear!" John's wife shouted. Yet, he didn't return this evening, he didn't appear the next day – the … **(Q2 pain)** truth was: he just never came back.

The mother grieved very much over her husband's … **(Q3 disappear)**. … **(Q4 near)** three years passed before she married again. Little Anne recovered from her … **(Q5 ill)** and grew up to womanhood.

When she was an adult, Anne got married to a man named John Smith, and after a few years had passed she also had a little girl named Mary. Anne still lived in the same house where they had lived when her father had disappeared. … **(Q6 happy)** once again had found its way into her family.

One night, on the anniversary of the disappearance of John Smothers, Anne's five-year-old girl was taken with cramp colic. "I will go downtown and get some medicine for her," said Anne's husband John. "No, no, dear John," cried his wife … **(Q7 desperate)**. "It's too … **(Q8 danger)**. You too might disappear forever, and then I'm all alone with little Mary." So John Smith did not go, and together they sat by the bedside of little Mary.

After a little while Mary seemed to get worse, and John Smith again attempted to go for medicine, but his wife would not let him. … **(Q9 sudden)** the door opened, and an old man with long white hair, entered the room. "Hello, here is grandpa," said Mary. She had recognised him before any of the others. "That's … **(Q10 possible)**," thought Anne. … **(Q11 confuse)**, she watched as the old man drew a bottle of medicine from his pocket and gave Mary a spoonful. She got well immediately. "Sorry for being late," said John Smothers.

0	artist ✓
Q1	careful
Q2	painful
Q3	disappearence
Q4	nearly
Q5	illness
Q6	Happiness
Q7	desperatly
Q8	dangerous
Q9	Suddenly
Q10	impossile
Q11	confused

Strange realities | 12

2 Linking words: Time and sequence

*Write down the recipe with the help of the notes below. Use the words in **bold** to link the sentence parts.*

Scary Halloween cookies

first	beat together butter and sugar in a large bowl
while	beat in the eggs and vanilla extract • add a few drops of food colouring to the mixture
before	stir the flour into the butter mixture • work into a dough using floured hands
after	divide the dough into two portions • leave to chill in the fridge for one hour
while	preheat the oven to 170 °C • line two baking trays with baking paper
after	roll the dough out on lightly floured work surface • cut shapes out with the Halloween cutters
while	place the cookies onto the baking tray • leave a gap between them
after that	bake for 12–15 minutes • leave on the tray for 10 minutes
when	cookies have cooled off • let your imagination run wild and decorate them
finally	serve cookies to guests who "trick or treat"

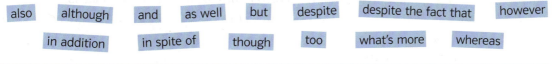

3 Linking words: Addition and contrast

a) The linking words and phrases below can be used to link similar ideas (addition) or contrast different ideas. Organise them correctly in the chart.

also   although   and   as well   but   despite   despite the fact that   however

in addition   in spite of   though   too   what's more   whereas

Addition	Contrast
also, and, however, in addition, too, what's more	although, as well, but, despite, despite the fact that, in spite of, though, whereas

b) Fill the gaps with a suitable word or phrase to link the ideas in the sentences.

1. ……*Despite*…… the fact that the shop was full of customers, they still helped us. They were very friendly ……*as well*…… .

2. The atmosphere is not as good as it used to be. ……*In addition*……, they've put their prices up ……*and*…… the staff is really unfriendly nowadays.

3. Sybil always comes to class on time, ……*although*…… her sister is late at least twice a week. ……*Despite*…… the fact that they live in one household, they are so different.

4. I think you can manage to win the race. It won't be easy, ……*whereas*…… . ……………………, the other contestants are quite strong.

5. I was told the hotel was very good. ……*In addition*……, it's reasonably priced. There are still plenty of rooms available ……*too*…… .

6. We have decided to go ……*although*…… the cost of the tickets. The Hendersons, ……*though*……, have planned to watch the match on the telly.

13 | Human rights

Human rights

TIP Prime Time 5: Unit 7 → S. 86

1 Language in use: Amnesty International

You are going to read a text about Amnesty International. Some words are missing from the text. Choose from the list (A–N) the correct part for each gap (1–11) in the text. There are two extra words you should not use. Write your answers in the boxes provided. The first one (0) has been done for you.

Amnesty International is a non-governmental … **(0)** (NGO) working to end human rights … **(Q1)** worldwide. It was founded by Peter Benensen, a British lawyer, who wanted to … **(Q2)** the situation of prisoners of conscience. These people are imprisoned, tortured and often … **(Q3)** because of their religious belief, their opinions, their ethnic origin, their sex, colour or language. They have not done anything wrong apart from the fact that they want to enjoy their human rights freely.

The most important strategy of Amnesty International is to organise letter-writing campaigns to put public … **(Q4)** on governments which are accused of … **(Q5)** human rights. They fight for the following aspects in particular:
- They want to free all prisoners of conscience.
- They want to make sure that … **(Q6)** prisoners get fair and prompt trials
- They want to … **(Q7)** the death penalty, torture and other cruel treatment of prisoners.
- They want to end executions without trials and "disappearances".

Today Amnesty International is a … **(Q8)** international NGO, which has more than three million sopporters, members and activists in over 150 countries and territories and it is still growing.

The organisation is … **(Q9)** non-political and completely independent in order to maintain its present status. The only thing that is common among all its members is that they … **(Q10)** in the importance of human rights and that they know that everybody has to help to stop human rights abuses, no matter where they might occur and who ever might be … **(Q11)**.

A	abolish *abschaffen*	G	improve	M	strictly	0	H ✓	Q6	C
B	abusing *Missbrauch*	H	organisation	N	violations *verstoße*	Q1	N	Q7	A
C	affected *betroffen*	I	physical			Q2	G	Q8	K
D	believe	J	political			Q3	F	Q9	M
E	cut	K	powerful			Q4	I	Q10	D
F	executed *hingerichtet*	L	pressure			Q5	L	Q11	?

Human rights | 13

2 Improving your word power

Use the words in the blue box to fill in the right expressions for the definitions provided below.

> discriminate against • employer • judge • privacy • slave • tolerate • torture • ~~violate~~

1. not to respect the rights of a person: *violate*
2. to accept other people's opinions and beliefs: *tolerate*
3. to use physical force and pain to make somebody confess: *~~judge~~*
4. a person who gives other people the opportunity to work: *employer*
5. a person who is bought and/or sold by his/her master: *slave*
6. to treat somebody badly e.g. because of his/her ethnic origin:
7. one's own space: *privacy*
8. a person who presides over a trial: *discriminate against*

3 A modern heroine

a) Read the following text.

Malala Yousafzai was born in 1997 in the Swat region of Pakistan. She became famous because she dared to campaign for the education of girls and for women's rights in the Swat Valley, where girls were partly banned from going to school. She started a blog on the internet to document the situation of girls in Northern Pakistan. Through this blog she became a celebrity and the Western media started reporting on her activities. She was even nominated for the International Children's Peace Prize and also for the Nobel Peace Prize. In October 2012 local gunmen tried to kill her but she survived. She was later taken to Great Britain to receive further medical treatment.

b) Now look at the definitions below and copy expressions with the same meaning from the text.

1. well-known: *famous*
2. to work in an organised way to reach a goal: *campaign*
3. schooling: *going to school*
4. to forbid: *banned*
5. to record: *reporting*
6. newspapers, radio and TV stations: *media*
7. proposed for: *receive*

4 Research modern heroes

Go on the internet and search for "CNN modern heroes". Then study some of the people and their initiatives presented there. Read the full stories and collect at least ten new words from each page you have read. Use a dictionary if needed.

14 | Growing up

Growing up

TIP
• Prime Time 6: Unit 1 → S. 6

1 Who's who?

a) Look at the family tree and complete the sentences below.

```
                    Alan ⚭ Michelle
        ┌──────────────────┼──────────────────┐
  Brad ⚭ Patricia    Thomas ⚭ Eliza    Peter ⚬⚬ Catharine ⚭ Albert
                    (died in 2004)
   ┌────┴────┐                              │              │
  Jill   Christine                       William          Rob
```

1. Brad is Eliza's ......brother-in-law...... .
2. William is Eliza's ....
3. Jill and Christine are William's ....
4. Jill is Catherine's ....
5. Alan is Rob's ....
6. Albert is William's ....
7. Peter is Jill's ....
8. Since 2004, Eliza has been a ....
9. Christine is Michelle's ....
10. Rob is Albert's ....

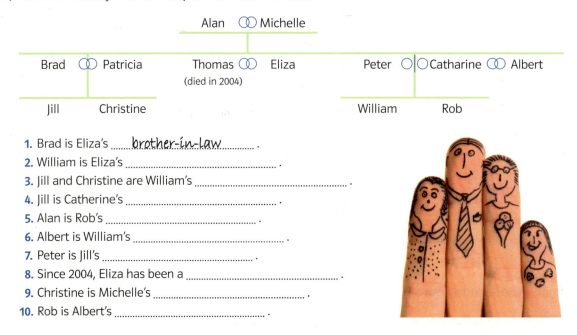

b) Write down more expressions for family relationships and make your own sentences with them.

2 A life story

Write down Simon's life story using the key words. Use linking words to turn the separate sentences into a text.

1. 1975 • born • Wales
   ......Simon was born in Wales in 1975.......
2. two years old • mother • new job • grow up • Switzerland
   ....
3. 19 years old • university • meet Alexa
   ....
4. for two years • go out with her • lots of arguments • split up
   ....
5. his mid-twenties • meet Rebecca
   ....
6. fall in love • within six months • get married • Wales
   ....
7. one year later • Rebecca pregnant • boy (Jason)
   ....
8. problems in marriage • Simon leave • get divorced
   ....
9. four years later • Rebecca • remarried • girl (Leyla)
   ....
10. Simon • single • visit Jason and Leyla regularly
    ....

3 How would you describe your best friend?

a) Find the synonyms in boxes A and B.

A	B
1. ambitious ☑ 2. cheerful ☐ 3. easy-going ☐ 4. generous ☐ 5. impatient ☐ 6. moody ☐ 7. optimistic ☐ 8. sensitive ☐ 9. sociable ☐ 10. trustworthy ☐	.... big-hearted .... confident .... compassionate ...1... determined .... emotional .... happy .... nervous .... outgoing .... relaxed .... reliable

b) Write the correct adjectives under the questions of the personality quiz.
c) Tick the appropriate boxes if you like this quality in your friend or not.

Personality quiz

1. Can you trust your friend with a secret?
   trustworthy, reliable
2. Does your friend sometimes pay for a drink?
3. Is it important for your friend to be successful?
4. Is your friend usually in a good mood?
5. Does your friend notice your feelings?
6. Is your friend happy one moment and then sad the next?
7. Is your friend usually not worried by things, no matter what happens?
8. Does your friend like to be with people?
9. Does your friend think the future will be good?
10. Does your friend become annoyed if he/she has to wait for something?

d) Describe typical situations in which your friend behaves in the following ways.

1. My friend is generous when *we go out together and have some fun*.
2. He/She is cheerful when ....
3. He/She is moody when ....
4. My friend is optimistic when ....
5. He/She gets impatient when ....

14 | Growing up

4 Language in use: Are teenagers the problem?

You are going to read a text about teenage problems and how they are seen by parents. Some words are missing from the text. Choose the correct answer (A, B, C or D) for each gap (1–10) in the text. Write your answers in the boxes provided. The first one (0) has been done for you.

When parents are together, they usually … **(0)** about raising teenagers. How do you get your teen to clean their rooms, handle … **(Q1)** that is rebellious or aggressive or make them more responsible? But does this really help us understand our children? Shouldn't we rather look at the problem in a … **(Q2)** light? In fact, growing up isn't that easy and today's teenagers face a number of problems we grown-ups are often not aware of.

At the very outset teenagers are struggling to come to terms with their body image and subsequently their identity. The sweet appearance of childhood gone, they are looking at strangers in the mirror with disproportionate limbs and acne. Many are … **(Q3)** to find a place in society and be accepted for what they are. This is the most important … **(Q4)** of their lives at this point and they are faced with a lot of anxiety and insecurity as they work around this.

Teenage stress … **(Q5)** with school work as they move higher. On the social front, a new horizon opens up – dating, partying, and … **(Q6)** out with friends. Teenagers are under much pressure to schedule time, prioritise work and achieve goals. Parenting teenagers at this stage is like walking on thin ice. Parents need to find the right balance. … **(Q7)** the teenager to get good grades, be well-behaved and responsible for themselves adds to the stress.

Every significant adult around the teen is attempting to mould them into some acceptable shape. The teen is … **(Q8)** ever able to do what they want to do with their lives. Frequently, teens arrive at decisions which conflict with their own skills or fields of interest. What we need is a clearer view of our parenting skills. We need to stop complaining and take … **(Q9)** for what we are exposing our teens to right now. Let them know that you don't always have all the answers and you too are not always right. Take their opinion and help them whenever needed. Most … **(Q10)**, let them know that you care.

		A		B		C		D	
0		complain		object		protest		oppose	
Q1		actions		manners		behaviour		performance	
Q2		similar		different		identical		varying	
Q3		struggling		wrestling		stumbling		engaging	
Q4		engagement		commitment		charge		task	
Q5		strengthens		increases		climbs		enlarges	
Q6		falling		spending		meeting		hanging	
Q7		Expecting		Believing		Insisting		Figuring	
Q8		mostly		badly		hardly		poorly	
Q9		responsibility		power		control		obligation	
Q10		seriously		mainly		specially		importantly	

0	Q1	Q2	Q3	Q4	Q5	Q6	Q7	Q8	Q9	Q10
A ✓										

Multi-ethnic Britain

TIP
• Prime Time 6: Unit 2 → S. 18

1 Finding useful expressions: Multi-ethnic Britain

Go through the words below and put two or more together. If you are short of ideas, go through the texts in the coursebook.

Black History Month, ...
....
....
....
....
....

2 Finding synonyms: Multi-ethnic Britain

Use the words in the blue box to fill in the right expressions for the definitions below.

> descend from • low wages • not confined • plantation •
> population • relationship • rent • statistics

1. to be a relative of: _descend from_
2. a big farm with crops like coffee, sugar or tobacco: _plantation_
3. the people of a country: _population_
4. tables and charts with data: _statistics_
5. the way in which e.g. two cultures are connected: _relationships_
6. the fee you pay for your flat: _rent_
7. low income: _low wages_
8. not limited: _not confined_

15 | Multi-ethnic Britain

3 Linking sentence halves

Choose sentence halves from the left side and match them with sentence halves from the right side.

1.	The first immigrants from the West Indies came to England in 1948, … **G**	A	because it was very profitable.
2.	Their intention was not to stay forever, …	B	because police protection was not adequate.
3.	The slave trade had contributed a lot to the prosperity of Britain, …	C	many had to accept low-income jobs.
4.	When the new immigrants arrived, …	D	they quickly founded their own newspaper.
5.	Even though some of them were well trained, …	E	because many immigrants knew hardly anything about their origin and history.
6.	The situation didn't change …	F	when more and more people started to arrive.
7.	Quite often they were exposed to harassment and abuse, …	G	because they wanted to find work and earn money for their families at home.
8.	As they had no say in the press, …	H	and run restaurants, bars, shops and nightclubs.
9.	Black History Month was introduced, …	I	they found it difficult to find suitable places to stay.
10.	Today many people with Caribbean background are very successful …	J	because many have a lot of money to spend today.
11.	They cannot be ignored by the advertising industry, …	K	but to go home to their families at some point.

4 Language in use: What is ethnic food?

You are going to read a text about ethnic food. In most lines of the text there is a word that should not be there. Write that word in the space provided after each line. Some lines are correct. Indicate these lines with a tick (✓). There are three examples at the beginning.

Ethnic food is an expression used to refer to dishes which are not — ✓ — 0
clearly mainstream in Britain. But what is mainstream **to** these — to — 00
days? Many British citizens have ethnic or culinary backgrounds — ✓ — 000
that are a far cry from what might to be regarded as British. — Q1
And yet, pizza or pasta or curry powder have been around for — Q2
such a long time that they can hardly be described as ethnic health — Q3
foods. With the arrival of immigrants from the West Indies mountains — Q4
or from India and Pakistan, a lot of their dishes became very — Q5
popular in Britain. Then in recent years Eastern and European — Q6
recipes have made their way into fashionable restaurants as well. — Q7
Not to mention American food stores which has made its way to — Q8
Britain in many different ways. It is not just the youth and culture — Q9
shock that has adopted the eating habits and the tastes that are — Q10
common in the US. — Q11
A clear indication that ethnic food has not been absorbed by many — Q12
British families is the fact that you can get ready-made meals in — Q13
their supermarkets with all sorts of flavours and based on a wide — Q14
variety of recipes, to be they Indian or Pakistani, Italian or — Q15
American, Polish or French. — Q16
So it is probably best to rethink the concept of ethnic food – and — Q17
just not enjoy the flavours – no matter where they come from. — Q18

5 Reading: An interview with Fatima Cummins

Read the text boxes below and put them in the right order.

1	Fatima:	Thank you.
2	Fatima:	Yes, of course! I'm 39 years old and was born in Notting Hill. Our family is from Trinidad, and I'm British. I'm a single mother with a 10-year-old son. I have a part-time job as a waitress at a pub in North London. I also sing a lot in our local school, and I sometimes help out in the after-school club. This is great fun with the kids from our neighbourhood.
3	Fatima:	No, not at all. Our community is very strong and there is hardly a weekend when we don't get together somewhere. Sometimes it feels like in the old days when we met in our front room. But things have also changed a lot. When I was young, nobody was well-off. So we shared a lot. It's not like that today, though. There are quite a few people in the area who have made a lot of money recently and that shows.
4	Fatima:	Well, I'm not sure. When I see them walk around with their smartphones and stuff I think they are pretty spoiled today. They cannot share the feelings we had when we were young. The situation is totally different. And sometimes I have the feeling that they are not aware of the history of their community. But … what really counts is that people have got used to us being around. That's probably the biggest change.
5	Fatima:	Hi, John, and thanks for the invitation.
6	Fatima:	Well, sort of. I mean I went to a normal school in the area, but I was also part of the Caribbean community. My friends were mostly from the West Indies. But later, when I started going out, I also met a lot of other people. Quite a common thing in London these days.
7	John:	But do you think that the younger generation has the same identity as yours?
8	John:	Sounds great, Fatima. Let's talk a little about your family and your background. You have grown up in a Caribbean community, is that right?
9	John:	Well, Fatima, can you tell us a little about yourself, please?
10	John:	Well, Fatima, thank you very much for this interview. It was great talking to you.
11	John:	This is John Garner and this week's programme of *Colourful Britain* with lots of interviews and music, music, music! This week the focus is on Trinidad. Our first guest is Fatima Cummins, whose parents were born in Trinidad. Hello, Fatima, and thank you for popping in to our studio this morning.
12	John:	What about traditions? Do you still share the traditions of your community or have these memories faded away?

11											

The Blue Planet

1 Vocabulary: Environment

a) Sort the words below into the three categories in the grid.

acid rain, animal welfare, carbon dioxide, climate, climate change, conservation, deforestation, desertification, disposable products, drought, earthquake, endangered species, exhaust fumes, extinction, fertilisers, flood, forest fire, global warming, greenhouse effect, nuclear energy, nuclear waste, ozone layer, pesticides, pollution, pressure group, rainforest, recycling, renewable energy, solar energy, typhoon, unleaded petrol, volcanic eruption, waste, wildlife

Normal phenomena in nature	Things that may harm the environment	Things that are good for the environment
carbon dioxide climate earthquake drought desertification endangered species extinction flood forest fire ozone layer wildlife typhoon	acid rain climate change disposable products deforestation exhaust fume pesticides pollution greenhouse effect nuclear waste/energy waste	animal welfare conservation recycling solar energy pressure group unleaded petrol

b) Complete the sentences with suitable words from task 1a.

1. The Mediterranean __climate__ is good for growing citrus fruits and grapes.
2. Scientists believe that there is a hole in the __typhoon__.
3. Some scientists say that man-made emissions of greenhouse gases are causing __greenhouse effect__.
4. The average cost of __unleaded petrol__ has risen by 7.3 pence per litre over the past two months.
5. Resist buying single-use, __disposable products__ such as bottled water and use a water flask instead.
6. Ploughshare tortoises, native to Madagascar, are one of the most critically __rainforest__ on the planet.
7. __Forest fire__ is destroying large areas of tropical rain forest.
8. They formed a __typhoon__ to prevent the local government from building a motorway near their homes.
9. The Hounslow __animal welfare__ Society rescues and rehomes hundreds of abandoned cats and other domestic animals each year.
10. Researchers say the results put __exhaust fume__ into the same category as passive smoking as a trigger for asthma.

2 Units of measurement

a) Study how to convert the most common imperial units of measurement to units of metric measurement.

Weight	Volume	Length
1 ounce = 28.35 grams 1 pound = 0.454 kilograms 1 stone = 6.35 kilograms 1 ton = 1,016 kilograms	1 pint = 0.568 litres 1 gallon = 4.546 litres	1 inch = 2.54 cm 1 foot = 30.48 cm 1 yard = 0.914 m 1 mile = 1.609 km

Temperature				
°F to °C: Subtract 32, multiply by 5 and divide by 9. °C to °F: Multiply by 9, divide by 5 and add 32.		°C 100 37 0	°F 212 98.6 32	Boiling point of water Body temperature Freezing point of water

b) Now convert the numbers in the two texts below.

A. My name is Michael and I'm from Kingston.
I am 15. I am 5 foot 2 inches tall.
I weigh 8 stone 9 pounds.
I had half a pint of milk for breakfast.
Today the weather is nice, about 56 °F.

I am __1.57__ (1) m tall.
I weigh __56.5__ (2) kg.
I had __0.2__ (3) l of milk for breakfast.
Today the weather is nice, about __13__ (4) °C.

B. My cousin Dirck is from Amsterdam.
He is 17 and he is 1.80 m tall.
He weighs 80 kg.
Today the weather is rainy in Amsterdam
and the temperature is 12 °C.

He is __5__ (5) foot __9__ (6) inches tall.
He weighs __12__ (7) stone __8__ (8) pounds.
Today the weather is rainy in Amsterdam
and the temperature is __53.6__ (9) °F.

c) Fill in the table with your own details and convert them to imperial units of measurement.

	Metric	Imperial
Your height	1,62 m	5,3 ft
Your weight	55 kg	121 pt
Size of favourite drink	1 l	0,2 gal
Today's temperature in your city	6 °C	42,8
Distance from home to school	8 km	4,9

d) Insert the numbers below into the following sentences and convert them into metric units.

3 gallons   88 °F   4 feet   20 miles   10 pints   ~~15 miles~~   107 °F   21-inch

1. The average raindrop falls at __15 miles__ per hour. — __24.135 km__
2. An average toilet uses __10 pints__ of water every time it is flushed. — __4 l__
3. Most people die if their fever reaches __107 F°__. — __4 70°c__
4. The amount of blood in the body of an average adult is __88 F°__. — __ne l__
5. Bamboo can grow up to __4 feet__ in a day. — __56__
6. A giraffe can clean its ears with its __21-inch__ tongue. — __79__
7. Polar bears can smell seal from __20 miles__ away. — __45__
8. Butter melts at __81°C__ approximately. — __107°F__

16 | The Blue Planet

3 Language in use: Global warming causes fish to shrink

a) *You are going to read a text about the effect of global warming on the world's fish population. Some words are missing from the text. Choose from the list (A–N) the correct part for each gap (1–11) in the text. There are two extra words you should not use. Write your answers in the boxes provided. The first one (0) has been done for you.*

The size of fish in the oceans is … **(0)**. A recent report from the University of British Columbia in Canada reveals fish may shrink by as … **(Q1)** as a quarter in the next decades because of global warming. The researchers conducted thorough tests on the effect of rising sea temperatures on the number and size of over 600 … **(Q2)** of fish around the world. They concluded that most fish are … **(Q3)** to shrink in size by 14 to 24 per cent by the year 2050. The most significant changes will be seen in tropical … **(Q4)**. The biologists explained there is less oxygen in warmer water so fish cannot grow at the … **(Q5)** they should. They added that many fish might migrate to cooler waters outside the tropics.

One of the lead researchers said, "We were amazed to see such a large … **(Q6)** in fish size. Marine fish are generally known to respond to climate change. But the unexpectedly big … **(Q7)** that climate change could have on body size indicates that we may be missing a big … **(Q8)** of the puzzle of understanding climate change effects in the ocean." He went on to say that human activities such as … **(Q9)** and pollution will worsen the problem. "Our work shows a very … **(Q10)** future for the oceans. It is very important to reduce greenhouse gas emissions and develop better fish management … **(Q11)** to adapt to these changes," he said.

A	decrease	G	overfishing	M	species
B	depressing	H	piece	N	tropics
C	effect	I	policies		
D	likely	J	rate		
E	migrate	K	regions		
F	much	L	shrinking		

0	L ✓	Q6	A
Q1	F	Q7	C
Q2	M	Q8	H
Q3	D	Q9	G
Q4	K	Q10	B
Q5	J	Q11	I

b) *Match the following parts of phrases that can be found in the article above. Then try to find them in the text.*

1. in the next	D	A	these changes
2. researchers conducted	F	B	of fish
3. over 600 species	B	C	of the puzzle
4. fish cannot grow at	E	D	decades
5. migrate to cooler waters	G	E	the rate they should
6. missing a big piece	C	F	thorough tests
7. overfishing and pollution	H	G	outside the tropics
8. adapt to	A	H	will worsen the problem

48

Making a difference

TIP
Prime Time 6: Unit 4 → S. 46

1 Finding synonyms and opposites

Find synonyms and opposites of the words and phrases below. Use a dictionary if needed.

Synonym				Opposite
rich	=	1. wealthy	↔	poor
to waste	=	2. to refuse	↔	accept
locate	=	3. to find	↔	search
earn money	=	4. to raise money	↔	loose money
strong	=	5. violent	↔	soft
prejuced	=	6. biased	↔	open-minded
promote	=	7. to support	↔	demotivate
positive	=	8. self-confident	↔	self conscies

2 Ways to evaluate

Write the following words into the right column. If you are not sure, check with a dictionary.

beneficial correct detrimental disappointing disloyal
encouraging fair frustrating helpful incorrect irresponsible
just loyal not right practical reasonable responsible right
true unfair unjust unpractical untrue wrong

Positive	Negative
correct, beneficial, helpful, fair, loyal, practical, responsible, reasonable, right, true, just	disappointing, disloyal, irresponsible, incorrect, frustrating, not right, encourage, unjust, unfair, unpractical, untrue, wrong

17 | Making a difference

3 Language in use: Make a Difference Day

You are going to read a text about Make a Difference Day. Some words are missing from the text. Choose the correct answer (A, B, C or D) for each gap (1–10) in the text. Write your answers in the boxes provided. The first one (0) has been done for you.

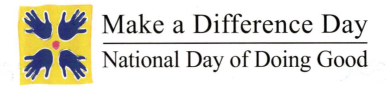

The … **(0)** thing about Make a Difference Day is that everybody can … **(Q1)**. The original idea was created by USA WEEKEND Magazine. What the organisers want is to help students bring out the best in themselves by … **(Q2)** others. Groups that participate organise local … **(Q3)** on various levels. Some might collect clothes for the homeless, others help old people in their … **(Q4)** or clean up parks or stretches of coast line.

Whenever help is needed in setting up such projects people can access the database on the website to find new ideas to get … **(Q5)**.

Many schools and colleges take part in these projects because they give their students the chance to … **(Q6)** meaningful activities in the community. This helps to improve the image of these organisations but it also helps to keep students … **(Q7)**. In addition, many activities offer great opportunities to … **(Q8)** learning beyond the classroom. Students get a chance to develop team strategies, to … **(Q9)** problem-solving skills and, most important of all, to … **(Q10)** self-esteem by helping others.

	A		B		C		D	
0	A	big	B	biggest	**C**	**great**	D	large
Q1	A	take place	B	take part	C	take on	D	take in
Q2	A	being helped by	B	reward	C	helping	D	underpinning
Q3	A	projects	B	projections	C	projectors	D	change
Q4	A	societies	B	communes	C	communions	D	communities
Q5	A	participated	B	initiative	C	involved	D	carried on
Q6	A	carry on	B	carry forward	C	carry through	D	carry out
Q7	A	motivated	B	moving	C	learning	D	going
Q8	A	extent	B	extend	C	extinguish	D	entail
Q9	A	acknowledge	B	acquire	C	acquit	D	acquaint
Q10	A	grab	B	grow	C	grade	D	gain

0	Q1	Q2	Q3	Q4	Q5	Q6	Q7	Q8	Q9	Q10
C ✓	B	C	A	D	C	D	A	B	C	D

Making a difference | **17**

4 Finding reasons why people may have problems

Read the words and phrases in the blue box and group reasons why people may experience difficulties in their lives. Look up the words and phrases you don't know. Some of them might fit into more than one category.

> not being able to pay the rent • ~~losing your job~~ • becoming unemployed • not being able to do hard physical work • having spent too much money • not being able to work in an organised way • having to care for sick or old relatives • working at a slow pace • being unable to afford heating • not being able to work in adverse conditions • being sacked • not being able to pay for loans • having to care for close relatives • being laid off • losing concentration • not being able to stand pressure • not being able to do complex jobs • not being able to move to another place • not being able to pay back the mortgage • not being able to cope with stress • being made redundant • not being able to do regular work • being separated from one's family • going through a divorce • divorce settlements • running away from home • violence in the family • not being able to lift heavy loads • being inflexible

1. problems in the job: *losing your job,*

2. problems in the family:

3. problems with housing:

4. problems with money:

5. mental problems:

6. physical problems:

Globalisation

Globalisation

TIP
• Prime Time 6: Unit 5 → S. 60

1 Globalisation shakes the world

a) *Read the following text on globalisation. Look for the words from the blue box in the text and underline them.*

> billing • economic growth • economic superpower • from boom to bust • industrial revolution • information technology • to lay off sb. • multinational company • outsourcing • overseas • payroll • post-war years • services sector • trade • white collar job

For Santosh, a tour guide in Bangalore, life is good. As a result of the IT boom, he has started his own web-based travel firm and sells weekend holidays to stressed-out IT workers.
For Dean Braid, a skilled car engineer in Flint, Michigan, life is not so good. He – and 28,000 other workers – was laid off by General Motors in 1999 and hasn't found a job since.

The accelerating pace of globalisation is having a profound effect on life in rich and poor countries alike, transforming regions such as Detroit or Bangalore from boom to bust – or vice versa – in a generation.

In economic terms, globalisation refers to the growing economic integration of the world, as trade and money increasingly cross international borders.

Globalisation is not new, but is a product of the industrial revolution. Britain grew rich in the 19th century as the first global economic superpower, because of its superior manufacturing technologies and better global communications such as steamships and railroads. But the pace and scale of globalisation have accelerated dramatically since World War II, and especially in the last 25 years. The rapid spread of information technology (IT) and the internet is changing the way companies organise production, and increasingly allowing services as well as manufacturing to be globalised.

In the post-war years more and more of the global production has been carried out by big multinational companies which operate across borders. Multinationals have become increasingly global, locating manufacturing plants overseas in order to profit from cheaper labour costs and to be closer to their markets. More recently, some multinationals like Apple have become "virtual firms" outsourcing most of their production to other companies, mainly in Asia.

It is not only the Western manufacturing industry that is under threat from globalisation. The services sector, which includes everything from hairdressers to education and software development, is also increasingly affected by globalisation. Many service sector jobs are now under threat from outsourcing, as global companies try to save money by shifting many functions that were once done internally. What China has become to manufacturing, India has become to the new world of business process outsourcing (BPO), which includes everything from payroll to billing to IT support.

The pace of change in the new world of globalisation can be frightening. A recent poll by Deloitte in November 2006 showed a sharp increase in the number of people who worry about outsourcing of white collar jobs in the UK.

The key question is whether the growing globalisation of the world economy will lead to a parallel increase in global regulation – and whether that would be good or bad for economic growth and equality worldwide.

(Steve Schifferes, *BBC News Online*, 21 January 2007; adapted and abridged)

b) Match the expressions you have highlighted in the text on page 52 with the definitions given below.

1. to lay off sb.	O	A office job which generally does not involve manual labour or the wearing of work clothes
2. from boom to bust		B action of buying and selling goods and services
3. trade		C amount of wages and salaries paid by a company to its employees
4. industrial revolution		D companies that produce services rather than physical products
5. economic superpower		E in or to a foreign country, especially one across the sea
6. information technology		F from increasing to decreasing
7. post-war years		G (sub)contracting of activities to free up money, personnel and time
8. multinational company		H years after a war (especially World War II)
9. overseas		I very powerful and influential nation in economy
10. outsourcing		J enterprise operating in several countries but managed from one (home) country
11. services sector		K process of sending bills for payment
12. payroll		L positive change in the level of production of goods and services by a country
13. billing		M rapid development of industry in Britain in the late 18th and 19th centuries
14. white collar job		N use of computers and telecommunications for storing, retrieving, and sending information
15. economic growth		O to discharge an employee

c) Recreate sentences from the article by taking one part from box A and one part from box B. Then check with the text.

A	B
• transforming regions	• everything from payroll to billing to IT support
• Britain grew rich in the 19th century	• first global economic superpower
• rapid spread of information technology	• from boom to bust
• business process outsourcing	• good or bad for world economic growth and equality
• poll by Deloitte in November 2006	• the way companies organise production
• global regulation	• worries about outsourcing of white collar jobs in the UK

1. Globalisation is transforming regions like Detroit from boom to bust.
2. ....
3. ....
4. ....
5. ....
6. ....

18 | Globalisation

2 Language in use: Outsourcing the news

You are going to read a text about outsourcing. In most lines of the text there is a word that should not be there. Write that word in the space provided after each line. Some lines are correct. Indicate these lines with a tick (✓). There are three examples at the beginning.

Text	Answer	Line
In an office in central **of** Bangalore, dozens of employees are arriving to	of	0
work on the night **line** shift. They are journalists employed by the world's	line	00
biggest news agency, Reuters. Their job is to cover US financial news.	✓	000
And they are working **at** overnight so that they can report company news	at *(news)*	Q1
live as it happens on the New York Stock Exchange – from India. But why	✓	Q2
in the world is Reuters covering over Wall Street from Bangalore? In a	in	Q3
word: salaries. These are Indian financial journalists **can** be employed by	can	Q4
Reuters for a fraction of the cost balance of employing a journalist at	✓	Q5
their New York office. Such a system has **only** recently become feasible –	only	Q6
as a result of the internet. Most of US companies **now** put out their press	no (of)	Q7
releases on the internet, and they all **pretty** use financial PR firms to	pretty	Q8
release their profit figures just as the stock market **all** opens. So Reuters	all	Q9
journalists in Bangalore can access the same basic information – in the	✓	Q10
same time frame – as their colleagues in New York **though**. And the	though	Q11
reduced cost of telecommunication means that the news is written	✓	Q12
in Bangalore can be sent around **whole** the world as quickly as	whole	Q13
the news written in New York – of key importance for a wire service,	✓	Q14
which **mistakably** depends on speed for its competitive advantage.	mistakably	Q15
Reuters' Bangalore operation is only one example of a broader trend in	✓	Q16
outsourcing by media organisations.	✓	Q17

3 Outsourcing vocabulary

Put the letters into the correct order and use the words in the sentences on the right.

1. **T E E X R N A L:** Mr Benning said that using an **external** provider was out of the question.
2. **O R N U T U S C O I G:** According to this article here **outsourcing** is growing by 20%–25% per year.
3. **T I V E S A C I T I:** Companies outsource tasks to concentrate on their core **activities**.
4. **A L T T E N:** We are working hard to build up a **talent** pool of suitable candidates.
5. **F S T A F I N G:** She argued that the shift to outsourcing would help cut **staffing** costs.
6. **W E R L O I N G:** The decision to outsource is often made in the interest of **lowering** costs.
7. **E L O D E V P I N G:** One of the benefits of outsourcing is the reduction of labour costs in **developing** countries.
8. **P E C O M T E:** Outsourcing allows companies to develop competitive strategies that will help them **compete** in the global marketplace.
9. **A L Q U I T Y:** Opponents of outsourcing claim that the **quality** of a service is usually worse when it is outsourced.
10. **P L O U N E M Y E D:** One criticism of outsourcing is that many people in developed countries become **unemployed** when their jobs are moved abroad.

South Africa

> **TIP**
> Prime Time 6: Unit 6 → S. 74

1 Find the right meaning

Match the words on the left with the correct definitions or examples on the right.

1.	landmark	C	A	making of products on a large scale using machinery
2.	stopover point	F	B	the language you use when communicating with a country's authorities
3.	endurance sport	D	C	a feature of landscape that can bee seen easily
4.	manufacturing	A	D	e.g. running marathons
5.	natural resources	G	E	the way in which governments or businesses act
6.	diverse origins	H	F	a place where you interrupt your trip
7.	official language	B	G	e.g. gold, oil, diamonds
8.	policy	E	H	coming from different backgrounds

2 The History of the African National Congress

Write a short text about the the history of the African National Congress. Use the notes below.

1912: formed to bring all Africans together as one people

In 1912 the African National Congress was formed to bring all Africans together as one people.

1944: Nelson Mandela joins

1944 Nelson Mandela joined the organisation

1950s: mass resistance to Apartheid starts

In the 1950s a mass resistance has started

1960: ANC banned

1960 ANC got banned

1961: beginning of armed struggle against the government

1961 was the beginning of the struggle against government

1964–1990: Nelson Mandela in prison for anti-Apartheid activism

Nelson Mandela got prisone for activism 1964-1990.

1990: ban against ANC lifted

1990 the ban got lifted.

1994: ANC win in first free South African elections with 62.6% of the votes

1994 ANC won election with 62,6% of the votes

1994: Nelson Mandela elected as first black president of South Africa

1994 Nelson was elected at the president.

1999, 2004, 2009: ANC wins three elections in a row

In 1999 2004 and 2009 ANC won elections in a row.

3 Language in use: *Cry freedom*

a) You are going to read a text about the movie Cry freedom by Sir Richard Attenborough. Some words are missing from the text. Choose from the list (A–L) the correct part for each gap (1–9) in the text. There are two extra words you should not use. Write your answers in the boxes provided. The first one (0) has been done for you.

Cry freedom is a thrilling movie … **(0)** Sir Richard Attenborough, a famous British filmmaker, which brings the troubled history of apartheid … **(Q1)** life. It is based … **(Q2)** a book by white journalist Donald Woods, who had met Steve Biko, a black South African student leader, who was later arrested, tortured and killed in police custody … **(Q3)** 1977. Biko was … **(Q4)** the opinion that black people in South Africa should not cooperate … **(Q5)** Whites. His radical views, however, did not stop him … **(Q6)** becoming friends with Donald Woods, who was a liberal newspaper editor in a small town in South Africa … **(Q7)** the time.

Originally Woods had been very critical of Biko's activities, but then he supported him and published important facts … **(Q8)** Biko's death. As all their activities were monitored by the police, Woods was put under house arrest, but managed to flee to London from where he kept campaigning … **(Q9)** the Apartheid system.

Richard Attenborough's gripping movie tells the story of Biko's life and death and of his friendship with Donald Woods.

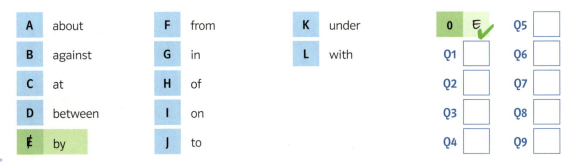

b) Look at the definitions below and copy expressions with the same meaning from the text.

1. affected by many problems: __troubled__
2. to take into custody: ……………
3. extreme: ……………
4. opinion: ……………
5. to prevent sb. from doing sth.: ……………
6. in the beginning, at first: ……………
7. to observe: ……………
8. to escape: ……………
9. to work for a political goal in an organised way: ……………

4 Language in use: Holidays

You are going to read a text about holidays in South Africa. Some words are missing from the text. Fill in the word which best fits each gap (1–8). Use only one word in each gap. Write your answers in the spaces provided at the end of the text. The first one (0) has been done for you.

… **(0)** in South Africa is very comfortable if you go to the right places.

For those of you who need a … **(Q1)** after a stressful period it seems the right country. Many hotels offer … **(Q2)** so that you can get in touch with your loved ones at home easily. If you want to treat yourself to something special you might want to get a room with an … **(Q3)** bathroom and a nice view. In some places they would even do the … **(Q4)** for you, which is especially handy when you have only a limited amount of clothes with you. If you care for a cup of coffee in the afternoon in your own room, you need not look for a specific place because coffee- and tea-making … **(Q5)** are standard.

If you enjoy the peace and quite of the countryside you might want to look for a place outside the cities, maybe even with a … **(Q6)** garden. Ample off-street … **(Q7)** is often provided.

And if you think that the country is ludicrously expensive, think again because in some places you can rent a self-contained cottage that sleeps up to six people, the ideal place for a … **(Q8)** to stay.

0	Travelling ✓
Q1	break
Q2	rooms
Q3	individual
Q4	laundry
Q5	spots
Q6	included
Q7	pos
Q8	a family

5 Word search: Kruger National Park

Find as many words related to the Kruger National Park as you can. There are six possible directions in which you'll find them (→, ←, ↓, ↑, ↖, ↙). There are 22 altogether.

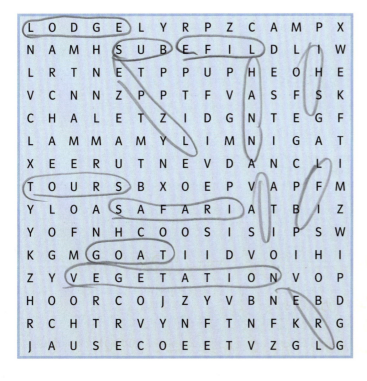

The world of work

TIP
• Prime Time 6: Unit 7 → S. 88

1 Working in an office

a) Complete the text below with suitable words.

agenda   appointments   arranges   customers   departments   factory   invoices

~~manufactures~~   minutes   paperwork   round   types

Gemma works for a company in Warwickshire which ...**manufactures**... (1) musical instruments. She works in the company's office building, opposite the .... (2) where the instruments are produced. Usually, she works at a computer, where she .... (3) letters and reports, and sends e-mails to .... (4) and business partners. She sends .... (5) to be paid to customers, and does quite a lot of .... (6), such as filing documents. Sometimes she is asked to show guests .... (7) the factory and tell them about the history of the company.

Gemma has to make .... (8) for her boss and put them in the electronic diary. She also .... (9) meetings for managers from different .... (10) and types the .... (11). Often she also has to attend meetings and take the .... (12).

b) Match the words on the left with the definitions on the right.

1.	to manufacture	D	A	routine work involving written documents
2.	minutes		B	building where goods are manufactured or assembled
3.	paperwork		C	device for fastening together sheets of paper with a staple
4.	invoice		D	to make articles on a large scale using machinery
5.	paperclip		E	summarised record of the proceedings at a meeting
6.	appointment		F	machine for making photocopies
7.	stapler		G	sb. who buys goods or services from a store or business
8.	customer		H	list of goods sent or services provided, stating the sum due
9.	filing cabinet		I	list of items to be discussed at a formal meeting
10.	department		J	arrangement to meet someone at a particular time and place
11.	photocopier		K	board with a spring clip at the top, used for holding papers
12.	agenda		L	division of a large organisation dealing with a specific area
13.	clipboard		M	piece of bent wire used for holding sheets of paper together
14.	factory		N	piece of office furniture with deep drawers for storing documents

20 The world of work

2 Compound nouns

Make compound nouns with one part of box A and one part of box B and use them in the sentences below.

A	B
~~arm~~ • black • brain • brief • filing • key • notice • over • time • wastepaper	basket • board • board • cabinet • case • ~~chair~~ • mail • sheet • storming • time

1. The manager sat in her ……… *armchair* ……… and watched the candidate suspiciously.
2. A man who was accused of ……………………………… has been arrested.
3. ……………………………… is the team's favourite technique for finding new ideas.
4. He poured coffee over his ……………………………… and now it doesn't work anymore.
5. The rules at their office are very strict – ……………………………… is not allowed at all.
6. It was found that he did not work the hours that were recorded on his ……………………………… .
7. If I were you, I'd look for the old reports in the ……………………………… .
8. I told him to put the invitation on the ……………………………… for everybody to see.
9. The contracts are in my black ……………………………… in the back of the car.
10. You can throw these papers in the ……………………………… . We don't need them anymore.

3 Word search: Vocabulary for attending meetings

a) Find the following words in the grid below. Make sure to look in all possible directions (→, ←, ↓, ↑, ↘, ↖, ↙, ↗).

calendar chairs clipboard colleagues date diary flipchart handout handshake marker meet OHP PowerPoint presentation presenter projector slides tables time whiteboard

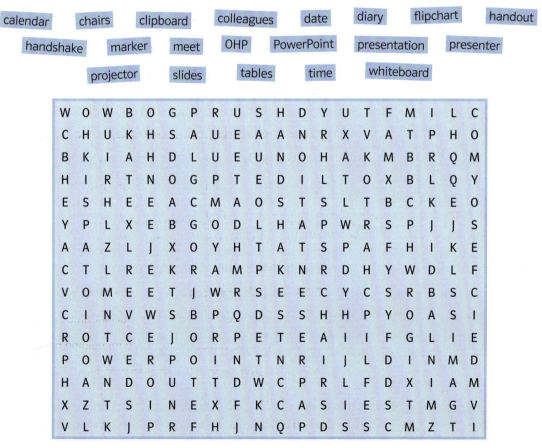

20 | The world of work

b) *Use some of the words from task 1a on page 59 in this invitation to a business meeting.*

Re.: Business Meeting on Thursday Jan 23rd at 9:00 a.m.

Dear ....colleagues.... **(1)**,
Thank you so much, all of you, for working so well as a team and being able to achieve last year's targets. I am sure there were valuable lessons learned from a few mistakes made, as mistakes are after all a chance to improve. This new year brings along new challenges and goals that cannot be achieved without the contribution of everyone on this team. In order to discuss this year's work plan and to highlight each team member's role, we'll .... **(2)** on Thursday, January 23rd, in the conference room at 9:00 a.m. The date has already been entered in our electronic .... **(3)**.
Team leaders are requested to give a 15- to 20-minute .... **(4)** that covers last year's achievements and next year's plans. Any additional agenda regarding resources and funding may also be included in the presentations. You may use the computer and .... **(5)** to show us your .... **(6)** or write onto the .... **(7)** directly.
In any case, please prepare a .... **(8)** each with the main ideas of your presentation.
I'm looking forward to seeing you all there!
Rachel

---

4 Language in use: Tips to boost your interview skills

You are going to read a text about how to make a good impression at a job interview. Some words are missing from the text. Fill in the word which best fits each gap (1–8). Use only one word in each gap. Write your answers in the spaces provided at the end of the text. The first one (0) has been done for you.

Even the smartest and most qualified job seekers need to … **(0)** for job interviews since interviewing is a learned skill, and there are no second chances to make a great first … **(Q1)**.

    Practise good nonverbal communication: Stand straight, make eye contact and connect with a firm … **(Q2)**. That first nonverbal impression can be a great beginning to your interview.

    Dress for the job or company: It is important to know what to … **(Q3)** and to be well-groomed. Whether you wear a suit or something less formal depends on the company culture and the position you are seeking. If possible, call to find out about the company dress … **(Q4)** before the interview.

    Listen: From the beginning of the interview, your interviewer is giving you information. If you are not hearing it, you are missing a major opportunity. Good communication skills include listening and letting the person know you heard what was … **(Q5)**. Observe your interviewer, and match their style and pace.

    Ask questions: Part of knowing how to interview is being ready to ask questions that demonstrate an … **(Q6)** in what goes on in the company. Asking questions also gives you the opportunity to … **(Q7)** out if this is the right place for you. The best questions come from listening to what you're asked during the interview and asking for additional … **(Q8)**.

0	prepare ✓

Q1 ....
Q2 ....
Q3 ....
Q4 ....
Q5 ....
Q6 ....
Q7 ....
Q8 ....

Famous speeches

1 Word formation

Complete the grid below.

Verb	Noun (thing)	Noun (person)	Adjective
to speak	speech	speaker	speechless
to free			
to	domination		
to		competitor	
to	protest		---
to		---	struggling
to	growth	grower	
to			talkative
to		---	successful

2 Language in use: Martin Luther King, Jr.

You are going to read a text about Martin Luther King, Jr. In most lines of the text there is a word that should not be there. Write that word in the space provided after each line. Some lines are correct. Indicate these lines with a tick (✓). There are three examples at the beginning.

✓	0
to	00
✓	000

On 4 April 1968 a bullet ended the life of Martin Luther King,
Jr., but it did not put **to** an end to his revolution. Since the 1950s
when Martin Luther King, Jr. started his campaign for Civil Rights
in America, the situation of African Americans has always changed — Q1
considerably. Eventually, the non-violent protest of the — Q2
Civil Rights campaigners has paid off. In the 21st century the — Q3
President Obama showed that it is possible to become an African — Q4
American President in the US. The campaigners of the 1950s and — Q5
1960s did not expect that the changes they longed for ever — Q6
would happen so quickly. — Q7
Today African Americans enjoy equal rights throughout it but in — Q8
the reality they are still disadvantaged. The prison population for example — Q9
still consists predominately of black and males. In general, black — Q10
Americans are less well-off doing than their white fellow citizens. — Q11
More black people join the US forces to combat unemployment — Q12
numbers and bear the burden in case of a war. — Q13
In his times then Martin Luther King, Jr. was also fighting for — Q14
economic rights of African Americans because he knew that legal — Q15
regulations alone cannot bridge the gap year between the rich — Q16
and the poor, between white and black America. — Q17
When he was killed in 1968, the Civil Rights Movement was lost — Q18
one of its charismatic leaders but there were others who continued — Q19
his struggle to gain for equality and recognition. — Q20

21 | Famous speeches

3 Working with synonyms

a) Match the words on the left with the definitions on the right.

1. to exploit	C	A	to arrange for sth. to take place later
2. to postpone		B	to be involved in
3. to dedicate to		C	to benefit unfairly by paying less than one should pay
4. to be engaged in		D	to come into view
5. to surrender		E	to devote time etc. to a cause
6. to persuade sb.		F	to be established firmly, to have one's origin in
7. to underestimate		G	to give up
8. to emerge		H	to give up sth.
9. to be rooted in		I	to have the same qualities as
10. to make sacrifices		J	to make sb. do sth. by talking them into it
11. to resemble		K	to regard sb. or sth. as smaller/less important than they are

b) Match the paragraphs on the right with the words on the left from task 1a and fill in the right forms.

to be engaged in	The cosmetics company was deeply involved in humanitarian activities. They ....are engaged in.... (1) educational projects in Africa.
	Everybody takes money for favours. This .... deeply .... (2) their local culture.
	The students gave up a lot of time to help underprivileged teenagers to learn how to read. They .... (3) a considerable amount of their spare time to this project.
	After the fight he was stronger than before. He .... (4) as a real hero.
	Some Western companies profit from the fact that they think they do not need to pay workers in developing countries fairly. They .... (5) the workforce there.
	She gave up smoking to be able to save the money for her daughter's education. She .... real .... (6) to help her daughter get a better education than she had.
	The children talked and talked to their parents until they gave up and allowed them to stay up late. It was surprising to see how they managed to .... (7) them.
	The author kept shifting the deadlines. He never finished at the arranged date. He was so disorganised that the publisher had to .... (8) the publication date.
	Peter and his sister look nearly the same even though they are not twins. With their dark eyes and their dark hair they .... (9) each other.
	They could not go on fighting against the Allied forces. They had to .... (10) quickly to save lives.
	Sometimes people do not take politics too seriously, but they should not .... (11) politicians because they can be very powerful.

4 Commenting on a speech

a) Study the yellow boxes below and form as many sentences as possible. Use the words in the blue box for your sentences as well.

Generalising
- ~~on the whole~~
- taking everything into account
- all in all
- all things considered
- for the most part
- in general
- generally
- by and large
- normally
- usually
- almost always
- most of the time
- typically

Liking
- What I really/most like about her speech is the fact that she … .
- I really admire him for what he said.
- I do respect her for … .
- The best part of his speech is … .

Clarifying
- What I really mean is, … .
- What I'm trying to say is that … .
- In other words … .

Adding an idea
- In addition, … .
- Furthermore, … .
- Moreover, … .

Disliking
- They dislike it when people start to … .
- She can't stand people who … .
- What I really hate is the way he talked about … .
- The worst thing is how she changes from … .

slow
fast
long
short
in the middle of a sentence
well-placed
skilful
high pitched
to raise one's voice
to join sentences
emotional
moving
inspiring
moderate
determined
to shout
even speed
varied
charismatic
to make pauses
to talk fast
to stop at the end of a sentence

Expressing opinion
- In my opinion … .
- From my point of view … .
- For me … .
- I think that … .
- I am convinced that … .

Comparing
- Compared with her speech, his one is rather long.
- He operates in the same way as … .
- She uses the same style as … .
- It seems similar to the speech by … .
- It is another way of … .

Contrasting
- Unlike Mr X, Mrs Y concentrates on … .
- His intonation was different from what I had expected.
- It sounds very different from … .

b) Write down eight such sentences.

Example:

> on the whole
> → On the whole I like Barack Obama's speech more than the speech by Churchill.

22 | Sports

Sports

TIP
• Prime Time 6: Unit 9 → S. 116

1 Do, play or go?

Decide between do, play or go and complete the sentences with the appropriate words. Mind the correct verb forms.

TIP
Use *play* with any competitive game that you can play, *go* with activities that can be done alone, and *do* with groups of related activities.

1. He used to ....*go*.... jogging every day when he was at school.
2. My parents and I love ....*playing*.... a good game of chess from time to time.
3. My sister ....*has been doing*.... gymnastics for over six years now. She won a lot of prizes too.
4. Last year we ....*went*.... windsurfing every day in our summer holidays.
5. He's quite the athlete. He ....*played*.... football, volleyball and basketball, too.
6. My friend ....*does*.... horse riding three times a week.
7. We could actually ....*play*.... a set of tennis while we're waiting for the kids.
8. My doctor thinks that ....*doing*.... aerobics twice a week is a good way of keeping fit.
9. His idea of the perfect holiday is to rent a boat and ....*go*.... sailing in Croatia.
10. He ....*does*.... athletics at his local track and field club.

2 Equipment, scoring and venues

Complete the table below with the appropriate equipment, the usual units for scoring and the typical venues of the different types of sports. Some words may have to be used more than once. Use a dictionary for words you don't know.

Equipment	Scoring	Venues
ball • bat • board • cleats • clubs • glove(s) • net • paddle • piece • protective pads (knee pads, shoulder pads) • puck • racket • stick • suit	down • game • half • inning • length • match • metre • move • out • point • quarter • set • strokes • yard	board • course • court • field • pitch • pool • rink • table • track

	Sport	Equipment	Scoring	Venues
1.	American Football	ball, cleats, protective pads	down, half, point, quarter, yard	field
2.	Athletics	clubs	metre	track
3.	Baseball	bat	yard	pitch
4.	Chess	board	game, set	~~table~~ board
5.	Football	pads, ball	match, out	field
6.	Golf	ball, stick	lenght, yard	field
7.	Ice hockey	puck, net	game	~~R~~ court
8.	Squash	racket, net	match	court
9.	Swimming	suit	metre, strokes	pool
10.	Table tennis	ball	set	table
11.	Tennis	net, racket	point, match	court
12.	Volleyball	net, ball	point, game	rink

Sports | 22

3 Extreme sports

a) Make sentences using one part from each box. Can you find a convincing reason for each sentence?

A	B	C	D
As far as I'm concerned … I honestly feel that … I strongly believe that … I suppose … I suspect that … I'd like to … I'd prefer … I'd rather … I'm convinced that … I'm pretty sure that … ~~In my opinion …~~ Many people think … The way I see it … When you consider that … Without a doubt, …	~~bungee~~ hang in-line marathon mountain rock scuba sky snow water	biking boarding climbing diving gliding ~~jumping~~ running skating skiing	1. ~~is the most exciting sport in the world.~~ 2. is far too dangerous for me. 3. is really fun to watch. 4. would honestly push me to the edge. 5. might be attractive for young people. 6. is probably rather expensive. 7. puts someone's life in danger. 8. needs a lot of training and practice. 9. needs a lot of courage to do. 10. has thrill and excitement in it.

1. *In my opinion bungee jumping is the most exciting sport in the world.*
2. hang gliding nice courage
3. in line skating is cool
4. marathon running very sporty
5. mountain bike is cool
6. rock climbing is very dangerous
7. sky diving is fun to do
8. water skiing like real skiing
9. ...
10. ...

b) Complete the sentences with words connected to the sports in task 3a.

1. The highest *bungee jump* took place in China from the 233-metre-high Macau Tower.
2. The greatest vertical distance covered in *rock climbing* in 24 hours is 8.88 km.
3. *in-line skat* got its name from the most important piece of equipment: the self contained underwater breathing apparatus.
4. The women's *marathon run* premiered at the 1984 Olympic Games in Los Angeles.
5. Otto Lilienthal built the first controllable *mountain bike* in the year 1890; he used wood and fabric.
6. The longest *scuba diving* race in the world was a ride from Canada to Mexico (4,344 km).
7. There are still ski resorts in the United States that do not allow *scuba diving*.
8. The numbers printed on the wheels of an *sky diving / inline skate* represent the diameter of the wheel and the hardness of the material.
9. On 20 May 2001, Michael Zang broke the world record for *sky diving* by completing 500 jumps in a day.
10. In 2012, *water skiing* set a new world record as 145 people were pulled behind a single boat.

4 Language in use: From the playing field to the laboratory

You are going to read a text about doping in sports. Some words are missing from the text. Fill in the word which best fits each gap (1–11). Use only one word in each gap. Write your answers in the spaces provided at the end of the text. The first one (0) has been done for you.

"It's not whether you win or … **(0)** but how you play the game." – That saying is used to define honour in sports. But today, many people question the honour of many top-performing athletes. They … **(Q1)** if these men and women have used banned substances to set records.

When people talk about sports doping, they often mean the use of anabolic steroids. Most sports organisations have banned the non-medical use of anabolic steroids, but some amateur and professional athletes continue … **(Q2)** them. They believe steroids help them when competing. Steroids are used to increase muscle strength but they also can … **(Q3)** the liver, increase cholesterol levels in the blood and stop production of the hormone testosterone. They can also cause personality changes. For example, steroid users may become angry for no reason. Some become … **(Q4)** on steroids: They feel they cannot live without them. Steroid users can become depressed and, in some cases, may want to take their own life.

In the 1990s, the International Olympic Committee organised a conference that led to the creation of the World Anti-Doping Agency, known as WADA. The conference was first organised after French police found banned substances at the world famous Tour de France cycling event. WADA is an independent agency that creates and enforces common anti-doping rules. It is made up of representatives of the Olympic movement and officials from around the world. It receives support from many … **(Q5)**, including the United States.

WADA says athletes have used substances to … **(Q6)** their performance for centuries. Ancient Greeks used special foods and drinks. Nineteenth century cyclists and others used alcohol, caffeine, cocaine – even strychnine, a strong poison. By the 1920s, sports organisations were attempting to stop the use of doping substances. But they lacked scientific ways to … **(Q7)** for them. Today, drug testing labs are very well equipped. It's a never-ending competition: Sports dopers are always looking for new substances and technologies to help them … **(Q8)** drug tests. And testers keep creating new tests for identifying the substances and fighting new technologies.

A lot of people ask themselves what is … **(Q9)** with doping. They say sporting events would be fairer if all of the competitors could openly take part in doping. Yet, helping athletes perform better is not necessarily good for their health. Experts believe it is wrong to say that … **(Q10)** doping would create an equal playing field. To do so would let economic resources and scientific expertise decide the results of sporting events. Anti-doping officials say they want to protect the integrity, or honour, of sports by guaranteeing what they call a level playing field. They want to ensure that … **(Q11)** who do not use banned substances have an equal chance at winning.

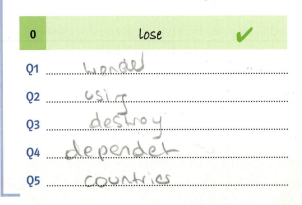

0	lose ✓
Q1	wonder
Q2	using
Q3	destroy
Q4	dependet
Q5	countries
Q6	enhance
Q7	test
Q8	pass
Q9	wrong
Q10	permitting
Q11	those

Beauty and fashion trends

TIP
• Prime Time 6: Unit 10 → S. 128

1 Vocabulary: Words beginning with *com-* and *con-*

Match the expressions on the left with the explanations on the right.

1.	to combine	I	A	ability to understand
2.	comedian		B	effect
3.	comfortable		C	to express one's opinion
4.	to command		D	being sure of oneself
5.	to comment		E	to communicate
6.	community		F	to take part in a contest
7.	to compete		G	entertainer
8.	complete		H	strong hard building material
9.	comprehension		I	to join into a single unit
10.	concrete		J	group of people living together or having something in common
11.	confident		K	to carry on with
12.	consequence		L	having all the necessary parts
13.	to consider		M	to give an order
14.	to consist of		N	person taking part in a competition
15.	to consume		O	providing physical ease
16.	to contain		P	to be composed of
17.	contestant		Q	to have within
18.	to continue		R	to think carefully about
19.	to convey		S	to use up

2 Word search: Adjectives to describe fashion

Find as many words as you can to describe fashion and write them down. When you're done there will be an additional adjective to fill in. Make sure you know what these words mean.

1. ....
2. ....
3. ....
4. ....
5. ....
6. ....
7. ....
8. ....
9. ....
10. ....
11. ....

P	U	S	P	S	A	U	P	A	R	S
I	A	P	H	T	M	P	E	R	S	H
S	W	E	E	R	A	I	T	I	T	A
T	E	C	N	A	Z	N	S	D	U	U
R	O	A	M	G	N	P	O	C	N	R
T	M	C	E	E	G	I	C	U	I	E
L	E	U	N	O	Y	R	K	L	N	A
I	H	L	A	G	O	I	I	O	G	T
N	A	A	L	R	N	N	N	U	L	O
G	R	R	E	E	K	G	G	S	U	I

23 | Beauty and fashion trends

3 Language in use: Beauty pageants

You are going to read a text about beauty pageants. Some words are missing from the text. Choose the correct answer (A, B, C or D) for each gap (1–10) in the text. Write your answers in the boxes provided. The first one (0) has been done for you.

Beauty … **(0)** for children have led to a lot of fierce … **(Q1)** over the years. People in favour of them claim that beauty contests can be a good learning opportunity for children whereas others are … **(Q2)** that they have a negative effect on young people in more ways than one.

The question simply is if there is any … **(Q3)** to be had when children as young as six participate in contests where they are … **(Q4)** not by who they are but by how they look. In … **(Q5)**, they are exposed to great pressure when the contest is under way. Whereas some think that these … **(Q6)** are good for the children's later careers, others warn that … **(Q7)** in such a contest might have long-term negative … **(Q8)**. Especially very young and sensitive children might not be able to cope with what they regard as a personal defeat. On the other hand taking part in such a pageant might help to launch a career in modelling or in the movie industry because it provides ample … **(Q9)** to be seen and photographed.

In many cases it is not only the child but also the parents who want to take part because they wish for their children to become rich and famous, something they might have … **(Q10)** out on in their own lives.

0	A	contexts	B	contains	C	contests	D	concurrences
Q1	A	critic	B	criticism	C	critique	D	shortcoming
Q2	A	convinced	B	convened	C	contained	D	contracted
Q3	A	beneficent	B	benefit	C	benefactor	D	befit
Q4	A	jugged	B	jagged	C	cadged	D	judged
Q5	A	ad-on	B	addition	C	atone	D	attain
Q6	A	possibilities	B	opportunities	C	experiences	D	attractions
Q7	A	falling	B	felling	C	failing	D	filling
Q8	A	effects	B	affects	C	artefacts	D	efficiency
Q9	A	attractions	B	experiences	C	possibilities	D	opportunities
Q10	A	lost	B	failed	C	missed	D	skipped

0	Q1	Q2	Q3	Q4	Q5	Q6	Q7	Q8	Q9	Q10
C ✓										

Beauty and fashion trends | 23

4 Language in use: My kind of style

You are going to read a text about style. Some forms are missing from the text. Choose from the list (A–N) the correct part for each gap (1–11) in the text. There are two extra forms you should not use. Write your answers in the boxes provided. The first one (0) has been done for you.

It is more than difficult to describe one's own style, ... **(0)** for someone who is not experienced at writing about such things. ... **(Q1)**, my style is a mix of everything I've got. And I have bought a lot of things over the years. That said, I don't care if my clothes are ... **(Q2)** the latest fashion. That is ... **(Q3)** not important for me. And that also explains why I don't really spend a lot of money on new outfits, ... **(Q4)** I spend very little on new things. I rather tend to recycle clothes I've got and combine them to reflect the mood I'm in.

When I go out and buy new things to wear, I ... **(Q5)** get what I think suits me best. However, I do sometimes listen to my friends and also tend to go for things that look good on other people. ... **(Q6)** some people change clothes several times a day, I generally don't. This is just not my way of doing things.

When I look at my wardrobe and I see something that is old and tattered, I would normally get rid of it sooner than later, but ... **(Q7)** I sometimes keep things which remind me of a special occasion when I wore it. As I reuse my clothes ... **(Q8)**, the fact that some of these things might have become outdated does not ... **(Q9)** bother me. It's the combination that counts.

For me choosing the right dress for an occasion is like dressing up. ... **(Q10)** to do that but it does not really reflect my personality ... **(Q11)** my habit not to spend too much on clothes.

A	apart from	G	it is fun	M	usually
B	especially	H	just	N	whereas
C	for one thing	I	moreover		
D	in fact	J	on the other hand		
E	in line with	K	quite often		
F	in spite of	L	really		

0: B ✓

Q1, Q2, Q3, Q4, Q5, Q6, Q7, Q8, Q9, Q10, Q11

5 Commenting on fashion issues

Complete the following sentences with the right forms of the words provided.

A. This jumper looks .... **(1 good)** on you, but it does not fit .... **(2 good)**. I think it is too .... **(3 wide)**. Such things are not worn .... **(4 wide)** any more. They are out of fashion.

B. I would appreciate it .... **(5 great)** if she did not wear this outfit again, even though it was designed by a .... **(6 great)** artist. The fabric, however, feels .... **(7 fantastic)**. I think she should recycle the pattern. It would go .... **(8 good)** with her coloured jeans.

Grammar

Present forms

1 **Present tense simple: Bilingual upbringing**

The present tense simple is often used for general statements.

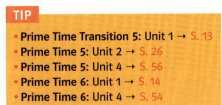

Highlight the present tense forms in this text.

Very often parents who have different first languages want to bring up their children bilingually – that means that the children grow up with both languages as their mother tongue.

Many parents report that their children have no difficulties learning two languages at the same time. In fact it can be a big advantage for their later lives because young children remember the sounds and the meaning of a word very easily. They get the feel for the language and this is something they will never forget.

However, these children often have enormous problems when they have to do grammar exercises in one of their mother tongues, because they have learned the language from their parents and do not know the rules of their first language.

2 **Present tense progressive: Mini dialogues 1**

The present tense progressive is used for actions that happen at the moment when you are speaking.

Underline the forms of the present tense progressive.

1. Mum: What are you doing in the bathroom? Come on or you'll be late.
   Lucas: I'm not doing anything. I am just getting ready, that's all.

2. Karen: Why are you pushing me all the time? Don't you see that I'm talking on the phone?
   Greg: Sorry, Karen.

3. Sue: Look at her. She is just ignoring me.
   Leah: Come on, she is just talking to the new boy from year 6. She has got a crush on him.

3 **Choose the correct simple or progressive form**

Circle the correct form. The first on has been done for you.

Usually **I am spending / spend (1)** my weekends with my friends. But this weekend I cannot be together with them because my cousin Peter from Australia **is staying / stays (2)** with us. He **is living / lives (3)** in Perth on the west coast of Australia. At the moment he **is visiting / visits (4)** my other cousins, but tonight he **is wanting / wants (5)** to go to a dancing competition. He **is liking / likes (6)** dancing because he **is going / goes (7)** to a school where he can do drama and modern dance. But I **am not thinking / don't think (8)** I can come with him because I **am not feeling / don't feel (9)** well. So he will have to go on his own. I hope he **is not minding / does not mind (10)**.

Present forms | 1

4 Questions and answers

Find the right questions in the present tense. Choose the correct simple or progressive form.

1. Question: ....
   (you – like – when – people – talk on their mobiles – on the bus – ?)
   Answer: No, not at all. I hate it. It's so embarrassing.

2. Question: ....
   (which – languages – you – learn – at school – ?)
   Answer: We all learn English and some of us learn Croatian or Turkish because this is their first language.

3. Question: ....
   (what – you – work on – at the moment – ?)
   Answer: Well, currently we are trying to organise a meeting of student representatives.

4. Question: ....
   (who – you – talk to – normally – ?)
   Answer: To my best friend at school. She always listens to me when I have a problem.

5 Negations in the present tense: Mini dialogues 2

Write short negative answers to the questions 1–4.

1. Question: Hi, I thought I would call you because you have not come in today. Are you working from home?
   Answer: Oh hi. No, I .... I'm on my way to the doctor's, I feel sick.

2. Question: Do you speak other languages apart from English and German?
   Answer: No, I .... I only speak these two languages.

3. Question: The weather here is fine. Is it raining where you are?
   Answer: No, it .... It's cold but sunny – a really nice day.

4. Question: Does he come from England?
   Answer: No, he .... He comes from a small village in Ireland.

6 Fill in the correct simple or progressive form

Complete the following text. Use the correct present tense forms.

In my spare time I .... (1 read) English books or I .... (2 work) in the garden. At the moment the flowers .... (3 come) out. It is such a nice sight. In the garden I usually .... (4 help) my mum. She .... (5 know) a lot about plants. In England many people .... (6 have) beautiful gardens with a nice lawn. Can you see the birds on the tree? They .... (7 sing) nicely. You can't hear this every day.

2 Past forms

Past forms

> **TIP**
> - **Prime Time Transition 5:** Unit 3 → S. 36
> - **Prime Time 5:** Unit 2 → S. 26
> - **Prime Time 6:** Unit 4 → S. 54

1 Past simple: Writing a report

a) Last week you had the chance to visit a conference for young people organised by the European Union. Use the notes in your diary to complete the report for your classmates at home.

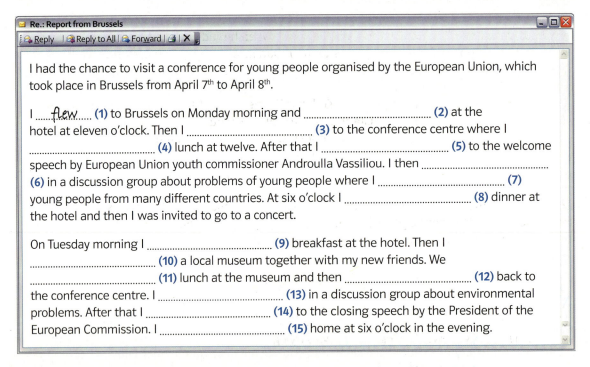

b) Think about what you did one day last week and write a report using the past simple.

Past forms 2

2 Past simple vs. past progressive 1: A mysterious story

a) Use the words in brackets in either the past simple or the past progressive form.

I ......**lost**...... (**1 lose**) my mobile while I .... (**2 run**) to catch the bus. While I .... (**3 go**) to school on the bus, I .... (**4 find**) somebody else's mobile phone on the floor. I .... (**5 try**) to unlock the phone when a girl .... (**6 appear**) next to me. She .... (**7 watch**) me when the phone suddenly .... (**8 ring**). Frightened, I .... (**9 drop**) the phone on the floor where it .... (**10 ring**) for some time. The girl .... (**11 wait**) for the phone to stop ringing and then .... (**12 step**) on it with her foot. She .... (**13 smile**) when the glass .... (**14 break**) and the screen .... (**15 go**) dead. I .... (**16 watch**) her without saying a word when the bus suddenly .... (**17 stop**) in front of the school. The girl .... (**18 jump**) out of the bus and .... (**19 run**) towards the school while I .... (**20 stare**) at the broken phone on the floor.

b) Why do you think the girl did this?
c) Invent a similar mysterious story of your own using the past simple and the past progressive.

3 Language in use: Past simple vs. past progressive 2: Inventions

You are going to read a text about inventions which were made by coincidence. Some forms are missing from the text. Choose from the list (A–K) the correct part for each gap (1–8) in the text. There are two extra forms you should not use. Write your answers in the boxes provided. The first one (0) has been done for you.

Cheeseburger: The cheeseburger might never have existed if not for an accident in the kitchen. In the 1920s, young chef Lionel Sternberger … (**0**) lunch when he suddenly … (**Q1**) a hamburger. He … (**Q2**) the charred spot under a slice of cheese rather than throw it away. The customer was delighted and the cheeseburger was born.

Super glue: Harry Coover, an employee at Kodak in Tennessee, … (**Q3**) for a temperature-resistant coating for jet cockpits when an assistant … (**Q4**) to tell him about an accident with the new material. Expensive lenses were ruined when they ended up glued together by the sticky substance. Coover … (**Q5**) work on the coating immediately and … (**Q6**) the following days to develop the perfect glue.

Chewing gum: In 1869, New Yorker Thomas Adams … (**Q7**) to make rubber for tyres using gum from chicle trees. One day he put a piece in his mouth to help him concentrate, and … (**Q8**) it was actually very enjoyable to chew.

A	ate	E	realised	I	was preparing	0	✓	Q3		Q6	
B	burned	F	stopped	J	was spending	Q1		Q4		Q7	
C	came	G	was looking	K	was trying	Q2		Q5		Q8	
D	hid	H	was melting								

2 | Past forms

4 Past vs. past perfect: The history of a great place

*a) Study the table below and remember how to use **after** and **before** to link two clauses.*

Earlier	Later
after + past perfect tense	Past tense
After settlers **had found** gold near Sacramento, many adventurers from Europe **came** to California.	
Past perfect tense	before + past tense
The town **had become** a violent trouble spot **before** the state **could** do something about it.	

*b) Now rewrite the sentences 1–4 combining the two clauses given. Use **after** and **before** to link them.*

1. Mission Dolores was founded in the 18th century by the Spaniard Fra Junipero Serra. – Sir Francis Drake failed to take possession of the area in 1579. **(after)**

2. The Spaniards sailed north to the Bay Area from Mexico to find new places to settle. – They took possession of Mexico. **(after)**

3. The first settlement was originally named Yerba Buena after a local herb. – The town was renamed San Francisco in 1847. **(before)**

4. San Francisco was a small town of about 1,000 people. – Its population rose to 25,000 in 1848–1849. **(before)**

Present perfect and other past forms

TIP
- Prime Time Transition 5: Unit 3 → S. 36
- Prime Time 5: Unit 2 → S. 26
- Prime Time 6: Unit 4 → S. 54

1 Present perfect simple or progressive 1

Complete the chart below.

A. I **have been reading** (1) the book for about an hour, but I **have not finished** (2) it yet.
B. I **have** just **arrived** (3). Now where are you? You wanted to meet at the cinema, didn't you?
C. I **have been trying** (4) to call you for more than an hour. Where **have you been** (5)?
D. Clare **has been working** (6) on her presentation since 7 p.m. I think she should stop now. It's too late anyway.

Simple	Progressive
2	1
3	
5	4
	6

2 Present perfect simple or progressive 2

Complete the sentences with the correct form of the present perfect tense.

1. My sister **has been learning** (1 **learn**) Croatian since she was two.
   She is very good at it now. However, when I started a year ago I found it very difficult.
   I **am giving up** (2 **give up**) now. I just can't do it.
2. I'm so sorry, I missed the train in London. I think I should have called you. How long **have you** been waiting (3 **wait**)?
3. Don't worry, I **have** just **had** _____
   (4 **have**) a phone call from Harry. He is all right.
4. Colin **has been working** (5 **work**) on his new book for about three months now, but he **hasn't finished** (6 **not finish**) yet. He wants to write two more chapters.
5. The storm **has uprooted** (7 **uproot**) all the trees in the road. The whole road looks very different now.

3 Present perfect with *for* and *since*

a) Read through the sentences of tasks 1 and 2 above and copy the ones that contain **for**.

1. I have been reading the book for an hour.
2. I have been trying to call you for an hour.
3. Colin has been working on his book for a month.

b) Ask "For how long?" and underline the **duration**.

Example:
> For how long have you been reading the book? – **For about an hour.**

3 Present perfect and other past forms

*c) Read through the sentences of tasks 1 and 2 on page 75 and copy the ones that contain **since**.*

4. Clara has been working since 7 p.m.
5. My sister has been learning since she was two.

*d) Ask "Since when?" and underline the **point of time**.*

Example:

Since when has Clare been working on her presentation? – **Since 7 p.m.**

4 Duration or point of time?

a) Tick (✓) the right box.

Time expression	Duration: For how long?	Point of time: Since when?
yesterday		✓
seven hours	✓	
two minutes	✓	
a week ago	✓	
Sunday		✓
several years	✓	
two months	✓	
Christmas		✓
November 3rd		✓
… I first met her		✓
six weeks	✓	
then		✓

b) Choose time expressions from the grid above and insert them in the sentences below.

1. She has not called since **Sunday**.
2. I have been waiting for her call for **seven hours**.
3. This has not happened since **I first met her**.
4. The sun has been shining **since yesterday**.
5. We have not been on holiday **since Christmas**.
6. We have been here **for two months**.

5 Signal words for the past tense and for the present perfect tense

a week ago   already   ever   just   last week/month/year
lately   never   yesterday   now   on September 15th   recently
since   so far   up to now   at Christmas

1. Signal words for the **past tense**: a week ago, last month, on September, yesterday, at Christmas

2. Signal words for the **present perfect tense**: already, ever, just, recently, now, lately, never, since, so far, up to now

76

Present perfect and other past forms | 3

6 Present perfect and other past forms 1: Facebooking

Complete the dialogue with the correct tense forms (present perfect simple, present perfect progressive, past simple)

Sam: ___Have___ you ever ___been___ (1 be) on a social network like Facebook or Twitter?
Clare: Oh yes, I ___have been___ (2 be) on Facebook for quite a while now. It's great.
Sam: When ___did you___ you first ___sign___ (3 sign up) on Facebook?
Clare: Well, I ___started___ (4 start) about two years ago. A friend of mine ___gave___ (5 give) me the address and ___showed___ (6 show) me how to do it. That ___was___ (7 be) it. And since then I ___have posted___ (8 post) the latest news about myself on the web.
Sam: And do you still like it?
Clare: Of course, otherwise I wouldn't do it any more.
Sam: So if we look at a typical day: How much time ___have___ you ___spend___ (9 spend) on Facebook last night?
Clare: After dinner I ___checked___ (10 check) my Facebook wall. And then I ___posted___ (11 post) the latest pictures. It ___was___ (12 be) great fun to read all the comments that ___keep___ (13 keep) pouring in. That's why I like it so much. I think it was ten when I ___shuted down___ (14 shut down) my laptop.
Sam: So we can say that you ___have spendi___ (15 spend) almost all your evening on Facebook.
Clare: Yes, I ___did___ (16 do).

7 Present perfect and other past forms 2: Complaining

Read through the e-mail and cross out the wrong forms.

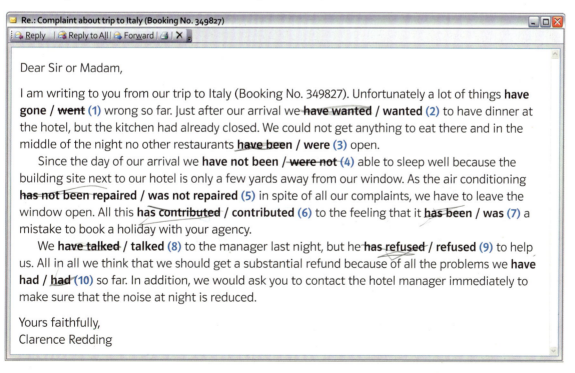

Re.: Complaint about trip to Italy (Booking No. 349827)

Dear Sir or Madam,
I am writing to you from our trip to Italy (Booking No. 349827). Unfortunately a lot of things **have gone** / ~~went~~ **(1)** wrong so far. Just after our arrival we ~~have wanted~~ / **wanted (2)** to have dinner at the hotel, but the kitchen had already closed. We could not get anything to eat there and in the middle of the night no other restaurants ~~have been~~ / **were (3)** open.
  Since the day of our arrival we **have not been** / ~~were not~~ **(4)** able to sleep well because the building site next to our hotel is only a few yards away from our window. As the air conditioning **has not been repaired** / **was not repaired (5)** in spite of all our complaints, we have to leave the window open. All this **has contributed** / contributed **(6)** to the feeling that it ~~has been~~ / **was (7)** a mistake to book a holiday with your agency.
  We ~~have talked~~ / **talked (8)** to the manager last night, but he ~~has refused~~ / **refused (9)** to help us. All in all we think that we should get a substantial refund because of all the problems we **have had** / ~~had~~ **(10)** so far. In addition, we would ask you to contact the hotel manager immediately to make sure that the noise at night is reduced.

Yours faithfully,
Clarence Redding

4 Future forms

Future forms

TIP
- Prime Time Transition 5: Unit 2 → S. 22
- Prime Time 5: Unit 2 → S. 18
- Prime Time 6: Unit 6 → S. 86

1 A holiday in Italy

a) Complete the e-mail with the words from the blue box in the correct form (present simple, present continuous or the "will" future).

> arrive • be • do • go • have • include • leave • let • ~~like~~ •
> look • not start • pick us up • see • take • visit

Re.: Italy's calling … ;)

Dear Joanne,

Do you want to spend your summer holidays with me again? I've got a great idea and I'm sure you **will like** (1) it!

I **am going** (2) to Italy in July, on a guided tour through the north of the country. Would you like to come too?

I know that you **are visiting** (3) your sister in Madrid in July to attend her wedding, but I'm sure she **will let** (4) you fly to Italy for a few days. The tour **doesn't start** (5) before July 20th anyway.

The itinerary is really promising. The tour **includes** (6) all the important cities in the north of Italy. Our plane **will arrive** (7) at Milan Malpensa Airport on the 20th. The tour guide **picks us up** (8) there and our coach **will take** (9) us straight to our first stop, Verona. Verona is known for Shakespeare's setting for *Romeo and Juliet*. There **is** (10) the chance to get tickets for a play at the 2,000-year-old Arena. Our next stop is Padua, one of the prettiest cities in Italy. Our hotel room **looks** (11) over one of the oldest botanical gardens in Europe. We **see** (12) the opportunity to walk around the old university building. And then Venice – everyone knows Venice. Venice is the last stop of our tour. After two days of sightseeing, our train back to the airport **goes** (13) at eight p.m. from Venezia Santa Lucia.

Have a look at their website www.touritaly.co.uk and let me know what you think quickly because I **leave** (14) the travel agent on Monday. I hope we **will do** (15) this tour together!

Take care,
Brian :)

b) Write a similar e-mail using the tenses correctly.

Future forms | 4

2 A school project in trouble

Reed and Agnes are having difficulties with their school project. Put the verbs into the correct form. Use the "will" future or the "going to" future.

Reed: I don't know what we ...**are going to do**... (1 do). We just haven't got enough donations for our Somalia project.

Agnes: I think we should advertise. We could put up posters across the school.

Reed: Yes, that's a good idea! That ...**will probably get**... (2 probably – get) our project more widely known. But do you think people ...**will come**... (3 come) to our classroom?

Agnes: Well, we could try to set up an information desk in the hall.

Reed: Yes, we could try that. I ...**am going to phone**... (4 phone) my dad to help us build a stall.

(on the next day)

Reed: Wow, you were right! I received four parcels this morning even before school started.

Agnes: See, I told you. We ...**will have**... (5 have) enough donations by the end of the week.

Reed: I think so too. But – what ...**will we do**... (6 we – do) if we get more parcels than we need?

Agnes: You can never have too many goods to send to Somalia.

Reed: Yes, but my mum ...**won't be able**... (7 not – be able) to get all the parcels in her car for the charity next week.

Agnes: If that's the case, we could ask my dad to help us too. I ...**am going to meet**... (8 meet) him tomorrow evening anyway. Don't worry, it ...**will all work out**... (9 all – work out) just fine.

3 Future situations

*Write what you would say in these situations. Use **will/shall**, **going to** or the present continuous.*

1. You have just prepared a cup of tea for a friend when she tells you that she doesn't take sugar. Offer to make her another one.
   ...I'm sorry! I'll make you another one....

2. Your teacher asks why you're leaving school early today. Explain that you have arranged to meet your uncle and aunt at the railway station.
   ...I'm sorry! It's arranged that I'm meeting my aunt....

3. A friend of yours is telling you about an exciting trip to Asia, which she has won. Ask her about the countries she's going to visit.
   ...Oh wow! Will countrys are you going to visit?...

4. You've been offered a role in a play and you have accepted. Tell your friends about it.
   ...Hey guys! I'm going to play a roll in a play!...

5. Your cousin lent you some money last week. Promise to pay him back as soon as you have received your pocket money.
   ...I promise I'll give it back to you soon!...

6. Your neighbour has turned the volume of her TV to the maximum. You get angry and ask her to turn it down.
   ...May you please turn the music down!...

5 Modal verbs

Modal verbs

1 Did this really happen?

> TIP
> • Prime Time Transition 5: Unit 5 → S. 67
> • Prime Time 5: Unit 6 → S. 84

a) Read the following story about a robber who behaved rather strangely. While reading, fill in suitable modal verbs. There might be more than one possible word for each gap. Try to find them all.

Just after eight o'clock in the morning a young man walked into a garage in Chicago. "This guy ...... *may/might/could* ...... (1) cause trouble," the employees thought. The man waved his gun at the employees behind the counter. "Open up the safe," he ordered. "And give me all the money." The employees looked nervously at each other. "We .... (2) do that," they told the robber. "Only our boss has the combination to the safe. We .... (3) open it without him. And he's not here yet."

The young robber .... (4) have expected such a problem. He got angry. "When is he coming in?" he asked. "We're not sure," said one of the workers. "He .... (5) come back some time before lunch." "But I .... (6) wait here all morning!" complained the robber. "I've got things to do." "We .... (7) call you when our boss gets in," said the employee bravely. There was a moment of tense silence. Maybe he .... (8) have said that. But to everyone's amazement the robber nodded his masked head. "Call me on my mobile as soon as he gets in," he ordered. "You guys .... (9) call me!" he warned the employees. "Otherwise I'm going to come back to shoot you."

Later that morning they did call the robber back. But they also phoned the Chicago police. And so the criminal was arrested as soon as he came back to the shop. "Put your hands up!" the police officer ordered. "Everything you'll say from now on .... (10) be used against you in court."

b) What do you think? Did this really happen?*

c) Rewrite the following sentences using suitable modal verbs. Compare the use of different modal verbs to put special emphasis on the sentences.

1. It is possible that the man causes trouble.
   ..... *The man may/might/could cause trouble.* ....

2. The employees are not able to open the safe because they don't know the code.
   ....

3. They are not allowed to open the safe without their boss.
   ....

4. It is possible that the boss will come back before lunch.
   ....

5. It would have been better if the employee hadn't said that they could call the robber back.
   ....

6. The employees have to stay at the back of the shop while the robber is being arrested.
   ....

2 Should have, would have, could have

Write six sentences about the story using each of the words below.

must(n't)   need(n't)   should(n't)   (don't) have to   had better (not)   ought (not) to

*Answer to task 1b: Yes. This story appeared in many newspapers.

80

Modal verbs

3 Language in use: Working in reality TV

You are going to read a text about working conditions in reality TV. Some forms are missing from the text. Choose from the list (A–J) the correct part for each gap (1–7) in the text. There are two extra forms you should not use. Write your answers in the boxes provided. The first one (0) has been done for you.

If your dream is to work in reality television, then there are some truths you … **(0)** come to terms with before you decide to start a career in that direction.

The hours in any television and film production jobs are often brutal. You … **(Q1)** realise that the production's needs come before those of the crew. Therefore you … **(Q2)** find yourself routinely working 12–18 hour days (sometimes longer).

Apart from that, the money you've heard so much about in Hollywood rarely makes its way to the crew. Salaries are often so low that junior crew members are … **(Q3)** pay for their living. And if you don't want to work for that little money, there are hundreds of other people who will happily replace you.

As a crew member of a reality show, you might see people with a lot of problems. Although it's human nature, you may … **(Q4)** to help these people. It's your job to put these moments on TV for the audience.

Unfortunately, working in reality television does not have a good reputation. Even within the entertainment industry itself some people think reality TV … **(Q5)** exist. Because you … **(Q6)** stand there and watch while real people go through difficult situations, people could start to judge you.

One way or another, you will … **(Q7)** to work through this on your own. The "thick skin" you've been hearing so much about as you start your career in Hollywood starts developing on shows like these.

(From: *About.com* by Phil Breman; adapted and abridged)

A	have to	E	need	I	should	0	✓	Q4
B	may not	F	needn't	J	shouldn't	Q1		Q5
C	might	G	not able to			Q2		Q6
D	must	H	not be allowed			Q3		Q7

4 DOs and DON'Ts in reality TV

If you fancy the idea of becoming a star in a reality TV show, you might find the following simple tips from casting show professionals useful. Take them to heart to make it to the finals.

a) Use modal verbs to turn the following keywords into whole sentences to express suggestions and recommendations.
b) Compare the use of different modal verbs to put special emphasis on the sentences.
b) Add your own ideas to the list.

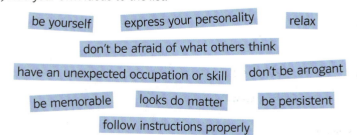

6 Conditional clauses

Conditional clauses

TIP
- Prime Time Transition 5: Unit 10 → S. 140
- Prime Time 5: Unit 10 → S. 134
- Prime Time 6: Unit 6 → S. 86

1 Zero conditional: General truths

The zero conditional describes something that is generally true.

Highlight the verb forms in the sentences below.

Example:

If the sun **rises** in the morning, the day **starts**.

1. If you want to become a famous author, you have to start writing texts at an early age.
2. If you want to learn more about how to use computers, it is not enough to play games on the net.
3. If you don't want to catch cold, don't open the window.

2 Zero conditional: Giving advice

Complete the e-mails below with the words in brackets.

Re.: No friends

Dear Agony Aunt,
I don't know what to do. I have no friends. So if I want to go out at the weekend, nobody ____wants____ (1 **want**) to invite me. I don't know what to do. I came to this town last month and I feel really lonely at times. Please help.
Karen

Re.: Re.: No friends

Dear Karen,
It's easier to make friends than you think. If you want to go out in the evening or at weekends for example, ____call____ (2 **call**) somebody you know and suggest to go out. If they don't have time to come with you, there ____will be____ (3 **be**) millions of other things you can do. Just do something and don't stay at home.
And if somebody is too shy to ask you out, you ____have____ (4 **have**) to take the first step. ____stay____ (5 **stay**) calm and ____be____ (6 **be**) patient, even if you are really lonely. It will soon work out.
Yours,
Donatella

6 Conditional clauses

3 Conditional 1: Real conditions

Conditional 1 sentences describe real or probable future situations.

Write if-clauses with the words given.

1. he • call • me – I • pretend • not to be • at home
   If he calls me, I will pretend not to be at home.
2. they • send • me • e-mails – I • not answer • them
   If they send me e-mails, I would not answer them.
3. you • water • the plants • too much – they • lose • their leaves
   If you water the plants too much, they will loose their leaves.
4. you • not • clear • the snow • in front of the house – somebody • fall • and • get • hurt
   If you don't clear the snow, somebody will fall.

4 Conditional 2: Unreal, but possible conditions

Conditional 2 sentences describe unlikely or imaginary situations.

Change one of these sentences into an if-clause and add the other sentence.

1. The rain stops. – We will go to the beach.
   If the rain stopped, we would go to the beach.
2. I lose my keys. – I will not be able to get into the house.
   If I lost my keys, I won't be able to get into the house.
3. Her parents have more money to spend. – She can come on holiday with us.
   If her parents had more money, she could come with us.
4. Paul will come to the cinema with us. – His uncle from Sweden does not come to visit them.
   Paul would come with us if his uncle did not visit them.

5 Conditional 2: What would happen if I missed the train?

Complete the text below with the words in brackets.

If I **were** (1 **be**) late for the train, the whole evening *would be spoiled* (2 **be spoiled**). If I *missed* (3 **miss**) it, I *wouldn't be able* (4 **not be able**) to meet my friends outside the concert hall. They would go in and if I came later, I *wouldn't be able* (5 **not be able**) to find them in the crowd. If that *happened* (6 **happen**), I *would try* (7 **try**) to call them on their mobiles. But I doubt it would work, because they would not be able to hear my call. If they *could hear* (8 **can hear**) their phones, we *would get* (9 **get**) together in the interval.

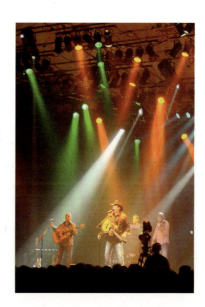

6 Conditional clauses

6 Conditional 3: Unreal conditions in the past

Conditional 3 sentences describe possibilities in the past that did not happen and that cannot happen any more.

Complete the sentences with the right forms of the verbs.

A. If I ___had been___ (1 **be**) there in time, I ___would not have missed___ (2 **not miss**) the flight.

B. If you ___had phoned___ (3 **phone**) earlier, we ___would have given___ (4 **give**) you the latest information. Now it is too late.

C. If I ___had known___ (5 **know**) that you wanted to join me on my trip, I ___would have booked___ (6 **book**) a ticket for you, but now there are no tickets left.

D. If there ___had been___ (7 **be**) enough lifeboats on the Titanic, more passengers ___would have survived___ (8 **survive**).

E. I ___wouldn't have become___ (9 **not become**) a waiter if my parents ___hadn't owned___ (10 **not own**) a small restaurant.

F. Had there not been so much snow, we ___wouldn't have had___ (11 **not have**) this accident.

7 Mixed conditionals

Complete the sentences with the right forms. Make sure that the sentences are meaningful.

A. I am terribly worried about their trip to the south. If I had been told about the journey, I ___would have told___ (1 **tell**) them not to go there. If anything ___had gone___ (2 **go**) wrong, we would have to organise a rescue party.

B. This present is going to be a big surprise for your grandma. If she ___had known___ (3 **know**) what we are planning, she would be rather cross, because she doesn't like dogs.

C. Running out of petrol on the motorway is quite embarrassing. If I ___had looked___ (4 **look**) at the dashboard, I would have stopped at the next petrol station to fill up the tank.

D. Our neighbours are very difficult. They don't like us making noise in the evening. If we did not turn down the volume of our stereo, they ___would have gone___ (5 **go**) mad.

E. We have been waiting for our guests to arrive. But if they ___had don't come___ (6 **not come**) in the next ten minutes, we will start serving dinner.

F. Her great ambition is to work for our local radio station. That's why she went there for a job interview. If they ___turned___ (7 **turn**) her down, she would be devastated.

G. Graham is certainly the best tennis player of our club. If he ___doesn't win___ (8 **not win**) all the matches, he will not join us for the party on the last day.

H. If you stop getting in touch with her, this ___will be___ (9 **be**) a clear sign that you are not interested in her any more.

Passive voice

1 Past participles: A burglary

TIP
- Prime Time Transition 5: Unit 8 → S. 105
- Prime Time 5: Unit 1 → S. 11

Insert the past participle forms of the verbs in brackets.

The only thing we know so far is that the door had been ....*forced*.... (**1 force**) open before the burglars entered the house. Once inside the living room was ....*devastated*.... (**2 devastate**). The furniture was ....*thrown*.... (**3 throw**) around, the curtains were ....*ripped*.... (**4 rip**) apart, the windows were ....*smashed*.... (**5 smash**). The whole house looked like a mess. Our forensic team was ....*called*.... (**6 call**) in to collect evidence. The samples were then ....*sent*.... (**7 send**) to the forensic lab to find out more about the burglars. In the kitchen a wallet was also ....*found*.... (**8 find**) which might belong to one of the suspects. That is the reason why we are sure that the burglars will be ....*caught*.... (**9 catch**) fairly soon. Pictures of possible suspects will be ....*published*.... (**10 publish**) in the next few days. The owners of the house were lucky because they were not at home when it happened. Otherwise they might have been ....*hurt*.... (**11 hurt**). As soon as we know more about the incident, the press will be ....*informed*.... (**12 inform**) immediately.

2 Passive voice: The basics

The passive voice is often used when people want to focus on the action.

Change the following sentences into the passive voice.

1. The thunderstorm destroyed the only bridge in the village.
   The only bridge in the village was destroyed by the thunderstorm.
2. The boys smashed the big bedroom window.
   The big bedroom window was smashed by the boys.
3. The earthquake damaged the church.
   The church was damaged by the earthquake.
4. Waiters in white dinner jackets will serve dinner.
   The dinner ~~would be~~ will be served by the waiters.
5. The band played a song by Vampire Weekend.
   A song by Vampire Weekend was played by the band.

7 | Passive voice

3 Passive voice: Shifting the focus

The passive voice is often used when people do not want to mention certain details.

Change the following sentences into the passive voice, but leave out unnecessary details.

1. Somebody opened the door and in came the president.

   The door was opened by somebody and in came the president.

2. Criminals set the castle on fire.

   The castle was set on fire.

3. In the course of the fire the flames destroyed valuable paintings.

   Valuable paintings were destroyed in the case of fire.

4. The fire brigade could not save the furniture of the house.

   The furniture of the house could not be saved.

5. Eventually the builders tore down the building.

   The building got eventually tored down.

4 Passive voice: Modal verbs

Change the following sentences into the passive voice, but leave out unnecessary details.

1. Somebody must switch off the lights before the performance starts.

   The lights must be switched off before the performance starts.

2. They must arrest the criminals before it is too late.

   The criminals must be arrested before it was too late.

3. The service personnel should wash the car before the guest of honour arrives.

4. The readers can return the books to the library on Sunday.

5. The organisers will change the text on the poster.

6. They could not close the front door because of the wind.

7. Users should remove the cover before changing the battery.

8 Indirect speech

Indirect speech

1 A Facebook chat

> **TIP**
> • Prime Time Transition 5: Unit 7 → S. 88
> • Prime Time 5: Unit 9 → S. 114

Read the e-mail from Stephanie about a Facebook chat she had with Della. Then complete the chat with what Della actually wrote to Stephanie.

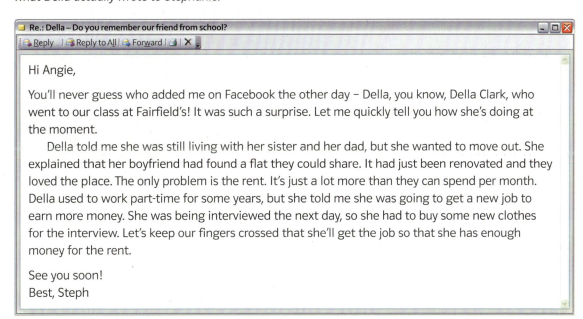

📧 Re.: Della – Do you remember our friend from school?

Hi Angie,

You'll never guess who added me on Facebook the other day – Della, you know, Della Clark, who went to our class at Fairfield's! It was such a surprise. Let me quickly tell you how she's doing at the moment.

    Della told me she was still living with her sister and her dad, but she wanted to move out. She explained that her boyfriend had found a flat they could share. It had just been renovated and they loved the place. The only problem is the rent. It's just a lot more than they can spend per month. Della used to work part-time for some years, but she told me she was going to get a new job to earn more money. She was being interviewed the next day, so she had to buy some new clothes for the interview. Let's keep our fingers crossed that she'll get the job so that she has enough money for the rent.

See you soon!
Best, Steph

Stephanie DuBois
11:19 – Hey Della, what a great surprise! Long time no hear. How are things?

Della Clark
11:20 – *Quite good actually. I'm still living with my sister and my dad but I wanna move out with my boyfriend, he found a flat to share.*

Stephanie DuBois
11:21 – Oh that's cool! What does it look like?

Della Clark
11:22 – *It has just been renovated! We love the place, there's just one problem*

Stephanie DuBois
11:23 – What problem? Why can't you move in soon?

Della Clark
11:24 – *The rent is too high. We can't spend that much money.*

Stephanie DuBois
11:25 – Oh I understand. Well, then I'll keep my fingers crossed for you! What are you doing in the afternoon?

Della Clark
11:26 – *I go shopping because I need new clothes for my job interview tomorrow*

Stephanie DuBois
11:27 – I'm sure you'll find the right clothes for the interview. Take care!

8 Indirect speech

2 A job interview

a) *Anele's company is looking for a new employee. Anele has just carried out a job interview with a candidate. Read the interview and complete Anele's report using elements of indirect speech.*

Anele: Good morning, Ms Shriver. Thanks for coming. Please sit down. Have you had a good journey?
Wilma: Yes, thanks. My car navigation system led me straight here. You can't miss the brightly coloured building really.
Anele: Yes, that's true. It does stand out quite a bit. OK, let's turn to our interview. First, please tell me about yourself.
Wilma: I was in customer service until last year. The last company I worked for was a phone company where I was handling incoming calls. I like connecting with people, so my sales went up 30 per cent within two months.
Anele: Why do you want this job, Ms Shriver?
Wilma: I want this job because it seems perfect for my skills and experiences, which include sales and marketing. Additionally, the team I would work with looks terrific. I understand that this is a company on the way up. I want be a part of this business as it grows.
Anele: And why should we hire you?
Wilma: It sounds as if you're looking for someone to come in and take charge immediately. My high energy and quick learning style enable me to address problems rapidly. I have the ability to stay focused in stressful situations. I'm confident I will be a great addition to your team.
Anele: That's all for the moment. Thank you very much for coming. As soon as we have finished talking to all candidates for the job, we'll get in touch with you. Goodbye!
Wilma: Thank you! I'm looking forward to hearing from you.

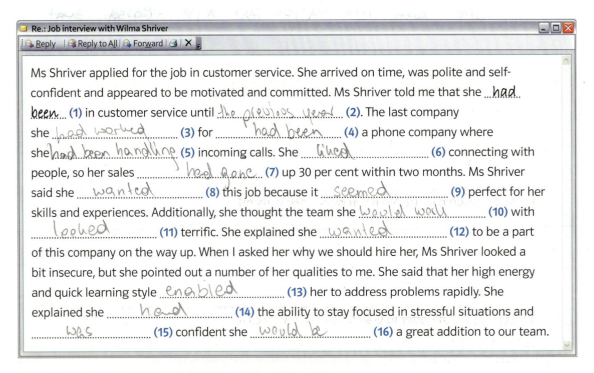

Re.: Job interview with Wilma Shriver

Ms Shriver applied for the job in customer service. She arrived on time, was polite and self-confident and appeared to be motivated and committed. Ms Shriver told me that she ...had been... (1) in customer service until ...the previous year... (2). The last company she ...had worked... (3) for ...had been... (4) a phone company where she ...had been handling... (5) incoming calls. She ...liked... (6) connecting with people, so her sales ...had gone... (7) up 30 per cent within two months. Ms Shriver said she ...wanted... (8) this job because it ...seemed... (9) perfect for her skills and experiences. Additionally, she thought the team she ...would work... (10) with ...looked... (11) terrific. She explained she ...wanted... (12) to be a part of this company on the way up. When I asked her why we should hire her, Ms Shriver looked a bit insecure, but she pointed out a number of her qualities to me. She said that her high energy and quick learning style ...enabled... (13) her to address problems rapidly. She explained she ...had... (14) the ability to stay focused in stressful situations and ...was... (15) confident she ...would be... (16) a great addition to our team.

b) *Carry out a job interview with someone from your class and write a report using indirect speech.*

Participle constructions

1 Using participle constructions to express reason or time

TIP
- Prime Time 5: Unit 4 → S. 52
- Prime Time 6: Unit 2 → S. 27

Read the script of an interview carried out by a police officer after an accident. Then complete the report below by using present participle constructions.

Police Officer: I understand you were involved in a traffic accident.
Jeff Thornton: Yes, it has just happened. I'm still quite shaken from the incident.
PO: Are you OK to answer some questions for me?
Jeff: Sure. I don't know how much help I'll be though.
PO: What can you remember from the accident?
Jeff: I was driving along Victoria Grove when suddenly a dog ran across the street.
PO: Did you run it over?
Jeff: No, because I saw the dog early enough, I braked hard and the dog ran away. But it seems that the driver in the car behind me couldn't stop. He was too close and so he crashed into the rear of my car.
PO: I see. But the side of your car seems damaged too. What happened there?
Jeff: As the guy behind me crashed into my rear, he pushed my car forward. I realised my brakes were not working anymore and so I couldn't do anything.
PO: How far did he push you?
Jeff: He pushed me right across to Earl Street. It was a dangerous situation since there is usually heavy traffic on Earl Street in the mornings. A car coming from the left couldn't stop in time and crashed into the side of my vehicle.
PO: Are you hurt?
Jeff: Yes, I feel a bit dizzy. But fortunately I had front and side airbags which protected me from serious injuries.
PO: Thank you very much for your cooperation, Mr Thornton. We'll come back to you soon.

Re.: Road traffic collision

__Driving__ (1) along Victoria Grove, Mr Thornton saw a dog __running__ (2) across the street. __Having seen__ (3) the dog early enough, he braked hard and the dog ran away.

Apparently the driver in the car behind Mr Thornton could not stop __having been__ (4) too close. He crashed into the rear of Mr Thornton's car, __pushing__ (5) the car forward right across Earl Street. __Realising__ (6) that his brakes were not working anymore, Mr Thornton could not do anything.

Mr Thornton found himself in a dangerous situation __sitting__ (7) helplessly in his car in the heavy traffic on Earl Street. Unable to stop in time, a car __coming__ (8) from the left crashed into the side of his vehicle. __Being__ (9) protected by front and side airbags, Mr Thornton has not been seriously injured.

10 | Participle constructions

2 Using present and past participle constructions to link sentences

a) Match the sentence halves to form meaningful sentences and copy them into your notebook.

1. The famous painting damaged by the fire … **E**
2. When Laura heard her son play the drums … **I**
3. The boy wearing the pink shirt … **D**
4. The sandwiches made by Peter … **H**
5. Having parked the car in the alley … **G**
6. The roses sent by my boyfriend … **A**
7. The man sitting next to my mum … **B**
8. I don't like clubs … **C**
9. She drew a picture of a horse … **J**
10. Having forgotten to change enough cash … **F**

A look beautiful in my dark blue vase.
B is dancing like mad.
C playing loud music.
D is her cousin.
E is being repaired.
F Lisa ran out of money in Turkey.
G my granddad was blocking the road.
H have all been eaten.
I she regretted having bought them.
J running across a field.

b) Link the sentences below using participle constructions.

1. Carlo rushed to help the victims. He had witnessed the accident only moments before.
   Rushing to help the victims, Carlo had witnessed the accident.
2. Iowa is known as the Corn State. It is one of the major producers of corn in the US.
   Known as the Corn State, Iowa is one of the major producers of corn.
3. The shop assistant stared at Fred. She was tapping her foot.
   Staring at Fred, the shop assistant was tapping her foot.
4. Misha looked at Natasha. Her face showed genuine concern.
   Looking at Natasha, Misha's face showed genuine concern.
5. The artist died penniless. He had been poorly paid for his compositions.
   Dying penniless, the artist had been poorly paid for his compositions.
6. Happily, the children danced around their igloo. It was made of hard-packed snow.
   Happily dancing around the igloo, which was made of chicoree.
7. Silvie opened her bag. She was looking for her wallet.
   Looking for her wallet, Silvie opened her bag.

3 Using relative clauses to replace present and past participle constructions

Change the sentences using who, which *or* whose *in relative clauses. Be careful with the tenses.*

1. The man crossing the road right now is our new neighbour.
   The man who crossed the road is our new neighbour.
2. Motorists driving under the influence of drugs or alcohol are likely to cause accidents.
   Motorists who drive under the influence of drug
3. Already sitting in his car, Freddy waved us goodbye.
   Freddy who sat in his car waved us
4. People with children suffering from leukaemia have a lot of worries.
   People with children whose suffer from leukemia
5. There has just been a terror warning for all planes flying to Syria this time tomorrow.
   There was a terror warning for all planes which fly to
6. Completed in 1937, the Golden Gate Bridge has become a famous landmark of San Francisco.
   The golden bridge which has been completed
7. Anyone found guilty of drug possession in Singapore faces the death penalty.

Verbs and their meaning

1 Let, make or have

*Rewrite the following sentences and use **let**, **make** or **have**.*

> **TIP**
> • Prime Time Transition 5: Unit 7 → S. 95
> • Prime Time Transition 5: Unit 9 → S. 126
> • Prime Time 5: Unit 3 → S. 38
> • Prime Time 5: Unit 4 → S. 56
> • Prime Time 5: Unit 9 → S. 121

1. My fence was damaged by the storm. It was mended on Friday.
   ...I had my fence mended on Friday.

2. Your dishwasher was broken. Somebody came round on Tuesday and repaired it.
   ....

3. You don't want to clear the table after dinner. Your little brother Jimmy should do it, it is his turn. When your sister starts putting away the dishes, you tell her that she should leave this to Jimmy.
   ....

4. Your father told you to clean the car. You had to do it.
   ....

5. You have no time to redecorate your flat. Somebody else has to do it for you.
   ....

6. Philip did not want to go shopping instead of watching TV. His mother forced him to do it.
   ....

7. Your little sister wants to climb up a tree. You think it is dangerous, but your father says you should give her the chance to do it on her own.
   ....

2 Verbs of perception

We use the *-ing* form when we focus on an ongoing action. We choose the infinitive if we want to refer to the action as a whole.

Choose the appropriate words below to complete each sentence.

> blowing   talking   go   trying   open   going

1. The detective saw the burglar .... the door, but it was too late to stop him.

2. Then he could not see him any more, he only heard him .... through the house.

3. He also saw the lights .... out.

4. He felt the cold wind .... against his face.

5. But suddenly he saw the burglar .... to open the first-floor window.

6. And then he heard him .... on the phone for more than minute.

11 | Verbs and their meaning

3 Dynamic and stative verbs: Examples

Dynamic verbs express actions and can be used in the simple and the progressive form. Stative verbs describe a state and are normally only used in the simple form.

Write the following verb phrases into the appropriate column.

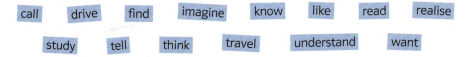

call   drive   find   imagine   know   like   read   realise
study   tell   think   travel   understand   want

Dynamic verbs	Stative verbs
1.	1.
2.	2.
3.	3.
4.	4.
5.	5.
6.	6.
7.	7.

4 Dynamic and stative verbs: Simple or continuous?

Circle the right tense form in the following text.

One day I **was reading / read** (1) a book about exotic holidays, when I **was suddenly realising / suddenly realised** (2) that I **had been finding / had found** (3) my perfect holiday destination. I **was knowing / knew** (4) immediately that this was the place I **was wanting / wanted** (5) to see. I **was really liking / really liked** (6) it because of the nice pictures in the book. I **was calling / called** (7) a friend of mine to tell her about this fantastic place, an island in the Caribbean. I **was thinking / thought** (8) she **would be liking / would like** (9) it as well. However, she **was not understanding / did not understand** (10) me correctly. She **was imagining / imagined** (11) that we would go there together. She **was thinking / thought** that (12) was the reason for calling her. When she **was telling / told** (13) me that she was happy to come with me I had to tell her that I **was wanting / wanted** (14) to go on my own. She **was nearly driving / nearly drove** (15) me crazy, but finally she **was understanding / understood** (16).

Nouns and articles

Prime Time 6: Unit 9 → S. 123

1 Plurals of nouns

a) Choose the appropriate words to complete each sentence and put them in the correct form of the plural.

tooth belief father-in-law formula life Dutchman fly mouse

1. We should respect people with different ......*beliefs*...... .
2. On board the aircraft were two ....
3. Some men get on very well with their ....
4. At the age of six most children start to lose their baby ....
5. The beach would be wonderful if it wasn't for those awful ....
6. Many teenagers just don't know what to do with their ....
7. Last night I saw two .... in our neighbour's garden. They were so cute!
8. For cosmetics firms the .... for their products are top secret.

b) Find ways to put the following words into the plural form.

1. music – ......*pieces of music*......
2. water – ....
3. information – ....
4. bread – ....
5. soup – ....
6. paper – ....
7. butter – ....
8. luggage – ....
9. sugar – ....
10. ketchup – ....
11. petrol – ....
12. milk – ....

c) Choose words from above to complete the following sentences:

1. They played his three favourite classical ......*pieces of music*...... for his birthday on the radio.
2. Thank you, these are really very useful ....
3. We offer three different ....: carrot soup, potato soup and our famous Bouillabaisse.
4. I bought two ....: a spicy one and a normal one.
5. Would you like one or two .... with your salad?
6. Can I have two .... , please? Without gas.
7. The tank of my car holds 60 .... That's more than my old car did.
8. I'll take two .... in my coffee, thanks.
9. How many .... will there be to take to the airport?
10. For this recipe, you'll need three .... Quite nutritious, that is.
11. He handed in the answers to the exam questions on three ....
12. When you go shopping get two .... , please.

12 | Nouns and articles

2 Training for a bikeathon: Using articles correctly 1

a) Tawnie is training to participate in a bikeathon. Every day she takes notes of her training and of the food she eats. Complete her diary entry with the appropriate words below, using **a/an** where necessary.

celery soup · egg · sandwich · roll · tomato sauce · apple · cereal · chocolate bar · spaghetti

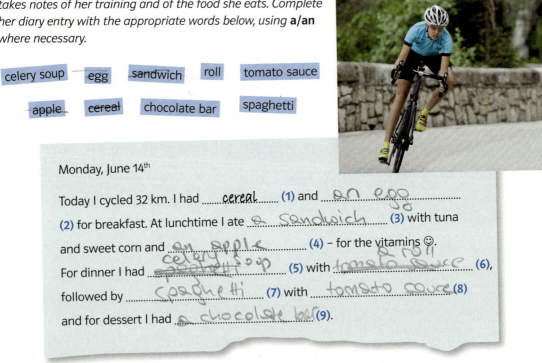

Monday, June 14th

Today I cycled 32 km. I had ......cereal...... (1) and ......an egg......
(2) for breakfast. At lunchtime I ate ...a sandwich... (3) with tuna
and sweet corn and ...an apple... (4) – for the vitamins ☺.
For dinner I had ...celery soup... (5) with ...a roll... (6),
followed by ...spaghetti... (7) with ...tomato sauce... (8)
and for dessert I had ...a chocolate bar... (9).

b) Do you lead a healthy life? Look at what Tawnie wrote and then write down what you ate yesterday.

3 Language in use: Using articles correctly 2

You are going to read a text about why teenagers should do sports. In most lines of the text there is a word that should not be there. Write that word in the space provided after each line. Some lines are correct. Indicate these lines with a tick (✓). There are three examples at the beginning.

There is a lot of **the** value in doing sports, either at school or somewhere
else. So, even if you think you're not a "sports" person you should
re-think that position.
First, the social benefits. It typically requires a team to do a sport. When
you practice everyday, play together, and have a patience to go through
the ups and downs of the success and failure, you bond. If you are shy or
have a hard time meeting people, then joining a sports team is an ideal
way to instantly meet and bond with the people.
Second, we need to consider the health benefits. Most the teens don't get
too motivated to simply "work out". However, most of them love a sports.
So, being on a sports team is a way to get the benefits of an exercise while
also having a good time. You may even get in the best shape of your life.
Finally, doing sports just makes you balanced. A lot of the teens think
because they are artistic or musical they can't do a sports. It doesn't fit
their image or something. But many actors, artists, and the musicians also
participated in athletics in a high school. Adding an activity like playing
the football or volleyball will make you that much more balanced.
And, the more balanced you can be, the more successful you'll
ultimately be in the life.

the	0
✓	00
✓	000
✓	Q1
a	Q2
the	Q3
✓	Q4
the	Q5
the	Q6
✓	Q7
✓	Q8
✓	Q9
✓	Q10
✓	Q11
the	Q12
✓	Q13
the	Q14
✓	Q15
the	Q16

Comparison of adjectives | 13

99 + 100

Comparison of adjectives

TIP
- Prime Time Transition 5: Unit 4 → S. 54
- Prime Time Transition 5: Unit 6 → S. 77
- Prime Time 5: Unit 8 → S. 110
- Prime Time 6: Unit 3 → S. 44

1 How to form comparisons

a) Choose five examples from the blue box and complete the tables below with the correct forms.

> weird • unusual • strange • famous • dead • bizarre • popular • few • tough • small • fascinating • smart • real • stylish • golden • favourite

Table 1: Comparisons with -er and -est

Positive	Comparative	Superlative
easy	easier	easiest
weird	weirder	weirdest
smart	smarter	smartest
strange	stranger	strangest
real ~~famous~~	~~realer famer~~ realer	~~famest~~ realest
small	smaller	smallest

Table 2: Comparisons with more and most

Positive	Comparative	Superlative
expensive	more expensive	most expensive
weird	more weird	most weird
smart	more smart	most smart
strange	more strange	most strange
real	more real	most real
small	more small	most small

b) Write down at least two adjectives which have no such forms.

dead   golden

2 Adjectives: Comparisons 1

Complete the text below with the right forms of the adjectives in brackets.

My favourite punk rocker is the ___weirdest___ (1 **weird**) guy I know to date. In spite of this he is the ~~popu~~ _most popular_ (2 **popular**) musician of his band. When you talk to him, he sounds ___bizarre___ (3 **bizarre**) because he speaks with an odd accent. But when you listen closely to what he says he comes across much ___smarter___ (4 **smart**) than expected. The way he plays the electric bass though is ___fascinating___ (5 **fascinating**) because he plays with his left hand. In a way this is not as ___unusual___ (6 **unusual**) as you might think. A lot of the ___most famous___ (7 **famous**) guitar and bass players have played with their left hands. For me he is the ___best___ (8 **good**) bass player around. And in addition, his outfits are ___stylish___ (9 **stylish**).

13 | Comparison of adjectives

3 Adjectives: Comparisons 2

Use comparisons to express the same ideas. Use the letters provided.

1. Samantha has got seven apples in her basket. Gilbert has picked five apples.

   There are f__ewer__ apples in Gilbert's basket than in Samantha's.

2. Helen passed the test with an A. Clare had a C in the same test.

   Clare's test was not as g__ood__ as Helen's.

3. On his way back he took the train from the station closest to his home.

   He took the train from the n__earest__ station.

4. He should get off the bus at the stop after this one.

   He should get off the bus at the n__ext__ stop.

5. The newscaster read the most recent news.

   The newscaster read the l__atest__ news.

6. This was her final sentence before she passed away.

   This was her l__ast__ sentence before she passed away.

4 Adjectives: Comparisons 3

Write down what these sentences mean. Use the words provided.

1. Ben is not as fast as Jamie.
   a) Ben __was slower.__ (slow)
   b) Jamie __was quicker.__ (quick)

2. Francis and Sue scored three points each.
   a) Francis __was good was as good as,__ (good)

3. Carl is twelve and Sally is twelve too, Patricia is fourteen.
   a) Carl __is younger than Sally.__ (young, Sally)
   b) Patricia __is as old as is older than Carl Sally__ (old, Carl and Sally)
   c) Sally __is older than Patricia__ (old, Patricia)

4. Ian has £200 in his bank account, Paul only has £50 altogether.
   a) Ian __has more money__ (money)
   b) Paul __has less money__ (money)

5. Diana often does not know what she has to do. Joan forgets even more. Only Justine is reliable and knows exactly what she has to do.
   a) Diana __is not reliable__ (reliable)
   b) Justine __is totally reliable__ (reliable)
   c) Joan __less reliable as Diana__ (reliable, Diana)

Adjectives and adverbs of manner and degree

> **TIP**
> • Prime Time Transition 5: Unit 6 → S. 77
> • Prime Time 5: Unit 8 → S. 110

1 News from the music camp

Greg is spending a week at a music camp. Read his e-mail to his parents and choose the correct alternative.

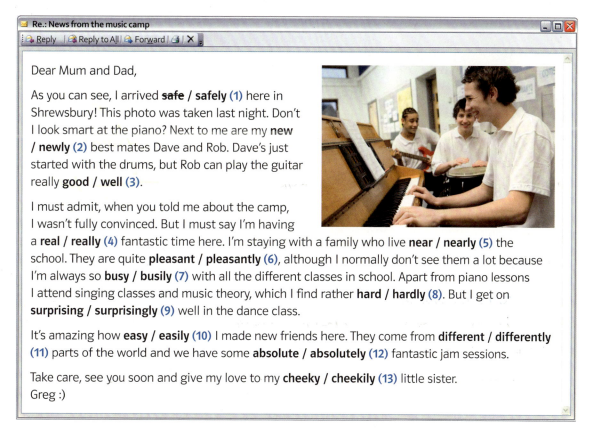

Dear Mum and Dad,

As you can see, I arrived **safe / safely (1)** here in Shrewsbury! This photo was taken last night. Don't I look smart at the piano? Next to me are my **new / newly (2)** best mates Dave and Rob. Dave's just started with the drums, but Rob can play the guitar really **good / well (3)**.

I must admit, when you told me about the camp, I wasn't fully convinced. But I must say I'm having a **real / really (4)** fantastic time here. I'm staying with a family who live **near / nearly (5)** the school. They are quite **pleasant / pleasantly (6)**, although I normally don't see them a lot because I'm always so **busy / busily (7)** with all the different classes in school. Apart from piano lessons I attend singing classes and music theory, which I find rather **hard / hardly (8)**. But I get on **surprising / surprisingly (9)** well in the dance class.

It's amazing how **easy / easily (10)** I made new friends here. They come from **different / differently (11)** parts of the world and we have some **absolute / absolutely (12)** fantastic jam sessions.

Take care, see you soon and give my love to my **cheeky / cheekily (13)** little sister.
Greg :)

2 Using adverbs correctly

a) Use the correct word from each pair to complete the sentences.

1. How ......**well**...... did the pupils perform in the oral exams?
   Amalie felt .... in her new dress.

   `good   well`

2. Simon looked .... at the gang of hooligans approaching him.
   As the gang had knives, it's no wonder Simon looked ....

   `nervous   nervously`

3. The coastal region was hit particularly .... by the tsunami.
   The inland regions were .... affected by the tsunami.

   `hard   hardly`

4. You're right, Dave has been .... depressed recently.
   Then they arranged the flowers .... in several vases.

   `pretty   prettily`

5. I haven't seen her .... so I don't know how she is.
   They're very busy so he's been getting home .... a lot.

   `late   lately`

b) Now explain the differences in meaning in your own words.

14 Adjectives and adverbs of manner and degree

3 Language in use: A musical evening

You are going to read a newspaper article about a concert given at a music camp for young people. Some words are missing from the text. Use the words in brackets to complete each gap (1–11) in the text. Write your answers in the spaces provided at the end of the text. The first one (0) has been done for you.

Last night the Shrewsbury teen music camp held its annual concert in the Theatre Severn Shrewsbury. To sum it up: It was a thrilling evening, even … **(0 good)** than last year.

The evening was opened by young Tobias Mitchell on his cello. He played … **(Q1 brilliant)** and amazed everybody with how … **(Q2 easy)** he mastered J. S. Bach's cello suites. We know that Tobias had worked … **(Q3 hard)** during the camp but with yesterday's performance he outdid himself.

The next piece was presented by Japanese student Amiko Kawatabe on her violin. She played Rimsky-Korsakov's "Flight of the Bumblebee", a very difficult piece. Amiko played … **(Q4 fast)** and she played … **(Q5 accurate)**. The moment the audience enjoyed … **(Q6 much)** naturally was the finale when Amiko's fingers … **(Q7 confident)** flew across the strings of her violin.

Every Shrewsbury teen music camp concert … **(Q8 traditional)** ends with the appearance of the camp's rock band. This year, the formation under 16-year-old band leader Greg Dobson called itself "The loud guys". They started … **(Q9 slow)** with a ballad written by music coach Mr Katkin. Some of the audience started dancing, but most waited … **(Q10 patient)** for the band to live up to their name. The grand finale was then the band's brand-new song "Only loud" which they played … **(Q11 terrible)** well – and loud.

0	better ✓	Q6	....
Q1	....	Q7	....
Q2	....	Q8	....
Q3	....	Q9	....
Q4	....	Q10	....
Q5	....	Q11	....

4 Position of adverbs

a) *Find and underline the misplaced adverbs, then rewrite the corrected sentences in your exercise book. Be careful: not all of them are in the wrong position.*

1. The police have been already informed about the attempted attack.
2. A new law was yesterday passed by Parliament.
3. Before you start using appliances, you must read the instructions carefully.
4. If you faster run, you might catch your bus.
5. Since the Norman Conquest Britain has been never invaded.
6. The conference begins tomorrow at 9 o'clock.
7. Recently a delegation of French industrialists visited China.
8. Floods have caused frequently serious damage to the village.

Adjectives and adverbs of manner and degree | 14

b) Put the adverbs in the right place in the sentences and write the sentences down. Sometimes more than one solution is possible.

1. We must finish our work. (today)

2. Children prefer junk food to healthy meals. (often)

3. Travelling long distances by ship is necessary today. (rarely)

4. Can the effects of global warming be observed? (everywhere)

5. The protesters believed in the success of their joint efforts. (firmly)

6. Our committee meets. (every week – on Tuesday – in the town hall)

7. We have got petrol to reach the next filling station. (enough – hardly)

8. The meeting will take place. (soon)

5 Adjectives and adverbs: Ancient civilisations

Complete the text by using the appropriate adjectives and adverbs (sometimes comparatives or superlatives) and other words from the selection below. Where necessary, form adverbs from the adjectives.

ago | amazing | ancient | as (2x) | ~~common~~ | developed | extreme | far | first | frequent | good | hard | high | human | in | mysterious (2x) | old | own | present-day | technological | used

It is ....*common*.... (1) knowledge that, dating back to 8,000 BC, Jericho is the .... (2) city .... (3) the world. Its walls were .... (4) built around 6,000 BC, and since then it has had many as they have .... (5) been destroyed during its history. What is less .... (6) known is that a .... (7) .... (8) culture existed in the Indus Valley between 2,500 and 1,600 BC in the region of .... (9) Pakistan. The cities .... (10) vanished without trace long .... (11), but while they existed their civilisation was .... (12) advanced .... (13). Their citizens even created their .... (14) writing, which was roughly .... (15) old .... (16) the hieroglyphic script of the .... (17) Egyptians. What is even .... (18) were the sewers they constructed to remove .... (19) waste and .... (20) water from houses. These cities remain .... (21) to this day as there is .... (22) any archaeological evidence that could provide .... (23) information.

103

15 Prepositions and phrasal verbs

Prepositions and phrasal verbs

TIP
• Prime Time 6: Unit 7 → S. 101

1 Prepositions of place 1

Write the phrases into the three columns of the grid.

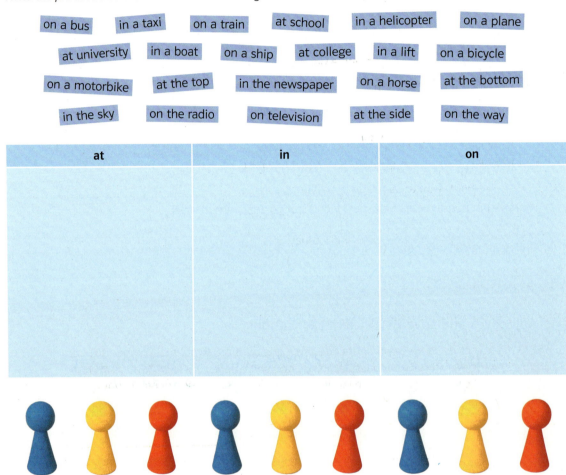

at	in	on

2 Prepositions of place 2

Underline the prepositions of place in the sentences.

1. My best friend lives in France now, not far from Lyon.
2. You can find the grammar explanation in a box at the bottom of the last page.
3. Her picture was printed on the cover of the magazine.
4. Unfortunately, they did not have roast beef on the menu.
5. When you go into the building you will see my office on the ground floor.
6. On the door to my office there is a sign with my name.
7. You can find our house easily, it's the red one at the end of the road.
8. But don't forget to turn right at the crossroads.
9. You can't miss our road, there is a small delicatessen shop at the corner.
10. On the wall next to it there is a big sign with the logo of our company.

3 Prepositions of place 3

Complete the sentences with appropriate prepositions of place.

1. I met Peter ....at.... the bus stop right in front of the entrance to the park.
2. As I could not find the ticket ....in.... my wallet nor ....in.... my pockets, I had to wait for Sarah ....at.... the entrance to the theatre.
3. The theatre is a beautiful building with a huge painting ....on.... the ceiling.
4. ....In.... the garden behind our house we have a small shed.
5. Our plane stopped ....at.... Edinburgh.
6. Can we meet ....at.... your office?
7. My aunt lives ....at.... 2 Willow Bridge Road in London.
8. I went to see her the other day, but she was not ....at.... home.
9. So I waited ....in.... the car, but she did not come.
10. ....At.... work we had a fire alarm today.

4 Prepositions of time

Complete the text with the prepositions from the blue box. Cross out the ones you have used. The first one has been done for you.

> at · at · at · at · at · at · at · at · at · by · by · during · for · from – to · in · in · in · in · on · on · on · until

In the morning Vince usually gets up ....at.... (1) 6:30. Then he has breakfast with his mum and his sister. He leaves home ....at.... (2) 7:30 to get to school ....on.... (3) time for the lessons. Sometimes he has to rush if the bus is not ....on.... (4) time. ....At.... (5) lunchtime he usually eats at school unless they have no afternoon lessons. Then he comes home ....at/from.... (6) 1:00 p.m. ....to.... (7) Tuesday afternoon he has a PE lesson ....at.... (8) 3:00 ....until.... (9) 5:00 p.m.

In the evening he would normally stay up ....by.... (9) 10:30 p.m., but .... (10) his birthday he can do whatever he wants. The only condition is that he has to go to school the next day.

.... (11) the weekend he can sleep much longer. He can go out and enjoy himself with his friends but usually he has to be home .... (12) midnight.

The school year starts .... (13) September, and .... (14) the year they have quite a few weeks off. .... (15) Christmas and .... (16) Easter they don't have to go to school .... (17) about two weeks. .... (18) the summer they have about nine weeks of holidays.

New Year's Eve is very special. The whole family stays up late and .... (19) midnight they celebrate the beginning of the New Year.

.... (20) the moment Vince is in year 5. He hopes to finish school .... (21) the time he is 18. .... (22) the future he wants to become an engineer.

15 | Prepositions and phrasal verbs

5 Phrasal verbs 1: Prepositions

Complete the following sentences with appropriate prepositions from the blue box.

> about • after • for • for • in • of • on • over • up • up • with

1. He does not know what to do. I think he can't cope ...**with**... the situation. We need to help him.
2. Talking won't help. It does not make sense to complain ...**about**... the situation.
3. I have not heard from her for a long time. I think we should get ...**in**... touch with her.
4. When my parents go out, I have to look ...**after**... my two little brothers.
5. The manager has a very important position. He is responsible ...**for**... the whole company.
6. I am too tired, I cannot do this any more, somebody else must take ...**over**... .
7. I think you should do something about your English. You have missed so many lessons and now you need to catch ...**up**... .
8. They waited outside the stadium, but Peter didn't turn ...**up**... .
9. If you are short ...**of**... money, it does not make sense to spend more than usual ...**for**... clothes.
10. Simon has been looking ...**on**... his pen for several days now, but he has not found it yet.

6 Phrasal verbs 2: Matching definitions

Match the two columns. If in doubt use a dictionary to find the right definitions.

1. to get on with sth.	C	A	to formally show that you are interested in a job
2. to work out sth.	D	B	to look after, to show your affection
3. to apply for	A	C	to make progress, to continue sth.
4. to accuse sb. of sth.	G	D	to look up sth. and study it
5. to get away with sth.	F	E	to spend time relaxing with sb.
6. to do research on	H	F	to escape without punishment
7. to figure out sth.	I	G	to claim that sb. has done sth. wrong
8. to hang out with sb.	E	H	to find the answer to sth., e.g. a maths problem
9. to come across sth.	J	I	to understand
10. to care for	B	J	to find by chance

15 Prepositions and phrasal verbs

7 Phrasal verbs 3: A quiz

Tick (✓) the correct meanings of the phrasal words below.

1. To **check in** means to …
   ☐ make sth. available. ☒ register on arriving at a hotel. ☐ to check sth.

2. To **get away with** means to …
   ☐ travel. ☒ break the rules without consequences. ☐ end or finish sth.

3. To **look after** means to …
   ☒ take care of. ☐ try and find sth. ☐ to follow sb.

4. To **put off** means to …
   ☒ change clothes. ☐ exclude sth. ☐ postpone sth.

5. To **show up** means to …
   ☒ arrive somewhere. ☐ get on in a group of people. ☐ put sth. where it belongs.

6. To **turn into** means to …
   ☐ make louder. ☐ go to bed. ☒ become.

8 Phrasal verbs and prepositions: An e-mail of application

Complete this e-mail of application with suitable phrasal verbs and prepositions.

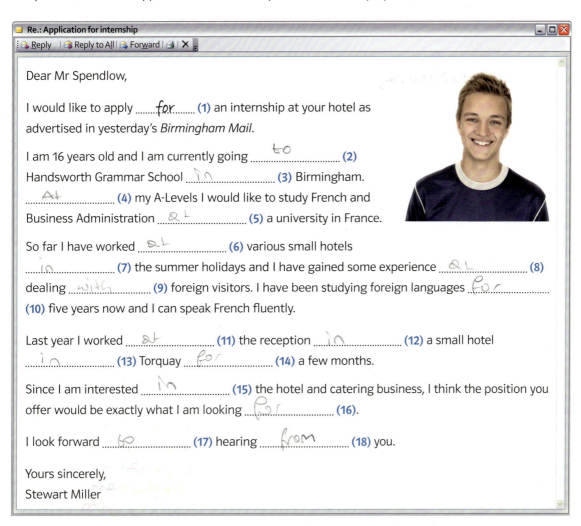

Re.: Application for internship

Dear Mr Spendlow,

I would like to apply ...for... (1) an internship at your hotel as advertised in yesterday's *Birmingham Mail*.

I am 16 years old and I am currently going ...to... (2) Handsworth Grammar School ...in... (3) Birmingham. ...At... (4) my A-Levels I would like to study French and Business Administration ...at... (5) a university in France.

So far I have worked ...at... (6) various small hotels ...in... (7) the summer holidays and I have gained some experience ...at... (8) dealing ...with... (9) foreign visitors. I have been studying foreign languages ...for... (10) five years now and I can speak French fluently.

Last year I worked ...at... (11) the reception ...in... (12) a small hotel ...in... (13) Torquay ...for... (14) a few months.

Since I am interested ...in... (15) the hotel and catering business, I think the position you offer would be exactly what I am looking ...for... (16).

I look forward ...to... (17) hearing ...from... (18) you.

Yours sincerely,
Stewart Miller

16 | Word formation

Word formation

1 Common noun endings: -ance and -ence

> **TIP**
> - Prime Time Transition 5: Unit 8 → S. 112
> - Prime Time Transition 5: Unit 9 → S. 125
> - Prime Time 5: Unit 6 → S. 85
> - Prime Time 6: Unit 3 → S. 45

Two common noun endings are **-ance** and **-ence**. Usually, their adjectives are made with **-ant** and **-ent**.

a) Look at the table below and complete the empty boxes with the help of the words given.

Noun	Adjective	Verb
accept**ance**	accepting	1. to accept
assist**ance**	---	to assist
(in)depend**ence**	2. independent	to depend
differ**ence**	different	3. to defire
dist**ance**	4. distant	---
exist**ence**	existing	5. to exist
innoc**ence**	6. innocent	---
intellig**ence**	intelligent	---
sil**ence**	7. silent	to silence
viol**ence**	violent	8. to violent

b) Use words from above to complete the following sentences.

1. What is the ......**distance**...... between Earth and Mars?
2. As an actor I love that special moment of ...**silence**... before the play starts.
3. What is the ...**difference**... between a dietitian and a nutritionist?
4. Does excessive .... in computer games encourage violent behaviour?
5. The new Bruce Willis movie was really exciting – nobody believed in his ....
6. A team of brain scientists has come up with the ultimate ...**intelligent**... test.

c) Go online and find more examples of nouns that end in **-ance** and **-ence**.

2 Turning verbs into nouns

One of the most common ways to change a verb into a noun is with **-ation**, **-ion** and **-ment**.

a) Look at the table below and turn the verbs into nouns using **-ation**, **-ion** and **-ment**.

Verb		Noun
to argue		1. argument
to compete		2. competitio
to decide		3. deciooment
to describe	+ -ation	4. descition
to develop		5. develoment
to encourage	+ -ion	6. encouragment
to excite		7. excitement
to explain	+ -ment	8. explanation
to improve		9. improvmen
to produce		10. producation

Word formation | 16

b) Use words from the table to complete the following sentences.

1. We had a big ...... **argument** ...... about whose turn it was to do the dishes.
2. My friends gave me a lot of ...... **encouragement** ...... when I was worried about my driving test.
3. You need to make a ...... **decision** ...... today: do you want to go to that school or not?
4. On the last day of the sports camp there was a bowling ...... **competition** ....
5. Despite the ...... **improvement** ...... , the results are still disappointing.
6. I gave the police a ...... **description** ...... of the thief.

c) Go online and try to find adjectives for some of the words in the table.

3 Turning adjectives into nouns

Many adjectives can form their nouns with *-ness*.

a) Use *-ness* to turn the adjectives into nouns. Then fill in the words that fit best.

| dark | forgetful | happy | homeless | lazy | lonely | rude | tired | weak |

1. ...... **Homelessness** ...... is a problem everywhere, not just in big cities.
2. His ...... **rudeness** ...... made me really angry.
3. When I woke up at 2:00 a.m. the house was in complete ...... **darkness** ....
4. At the job interview, I was asked about my strengths and ...... **weaknesses** ....
5. I used to find his ...... **laziness** ...... funny, but now it really annoys me.
6. ...... **Tiredness** ...... can cause accidents, so drivers should rest during long car journeys.

b) Write sentences of your own with the rest of the words.

4 Negatives

a) Look at the two tables below and study the words. Find out which word types (*nouns, verbs* or *adjectives*) these words belong to. Mark them in three different colours.

un-	in-	dis-	im-
unexpected	**in**accurate	to **dis**like	**im**possible
unbelievable	**in**appropriate	to **dis**agree	**im**polite
unknown	**in**efficient	**dis**belief	**im**perfect
unable	**in**capable	**dis**honest	**im**patient

il-	ir-	mis-	-less
illegal	**ir**regular	to **mis**behave	care**less**
illiterate	**ir**responsible	to **mis**understand	harm**less**
illogical	**ir**rational	to **mis**spell	help**less**
illegible	**ir**resistible	to **mis**use	end**less**

b) Use words from above to complete the following sentences:

1. The politician was accused of being ...... **dishonest** ....
2. His story was so ...... **unbelievable** ...... I thought he was crazy.
3. He's invited me to his party. It would be ...... **impolite** ...... to say no.
4. That's not what I said! You've completely ...... **misunderstood** ...... me.
5. My dog is really ...... **harmless** ...... I promise he won't bite.
6. In many states it's ...... **illegal** ...... to smoke in public places nowadays.

17 Relative clauses

Relative clauses

> **TIP**
> • Prime Time Transition 5: Unit 9 → S. 128
> • Prime Time 5: Unit 3 → S. 40

1 Non-defining relative clauses: Famous Australians

a) Use the information in the table to write sentences about these six famous Australians.

Name	Occupation	Information 1	Information 2
Hugh Jackman	actor	born on 12 October 1969 in Sydney	doesn't smoke in real life and finds it very difficult to smoke in movies
Kylie Minogue	singer	first big hit in 1989 was called "I should be so lucky"	launched her own social network called KylieKonnect in 2007
Rupert Murdoch	media mogul	was a friend of US President Ronald Reagan	started with a local newspaper and expanded his empire in the UK, Asia and the USA
Cathy Freeman	runner	lit the Olympic flame at the 2000 Sydney Olympics	announced her retirement from competitive running in 2003
Billy Hughes	Australia's seventh Prime Minister	nickname was "Little Digger"	changed parties five times over his parliamentary career of 51 years
Dame Edna Everage	fictitious character	played by comedian Barry Humphries	has been mentioned on *The Simpsons* three times

1. *Actor Hugh Jackman, who was born on 12 October 1969 in Sydney, doesn't smoke in real life and finds it very difficult to smoke in movies.*
2. ....
3. ....
4. ....
5. ....
6. ....

b) Write similar sentences about famous people from your own country or region.

2 Defining or non-defining relative clause?

Read the sentences. Then decide which option is correct and explain why.

1. My brother, who lives in Canberra, is a music journalist.
   a) I have one brother.
   b) I have more than one brother.

2. The cyclists who tested positive for doping were suspended.
   a) All the cyclists tested positive for doping.
   b) Some cyclists didn't test positive for doping.

3. HD video cameras, which are very expensive, have a better image quality.
   a) All HD video cameras are very expensive.
   b) Some HD video cameras are cheap.

4. The students at this school who arrive late for class will be suspended.
   a) Only some students arrive late for class.
   b) All the students in the school arrive late for class.

5. The company president who works in London is moving to Sydney.
   a) There is only one company president.
   b) There is more than one company president.

3 The place where, the day when and the reason why

Complete the blanks with information that is true for you.

1. ....Easter Sunday.... is the day in my country when ....children look for Easter eggs....
2. .... is a person I know who ....
3. .... is the room in my house where ....
4. .... is a time of year when ....
5. .... is the part of my town where ....
6. .... is the reason why ....

4 Contact clauses: The shortest possible form

*Rewrite the sentences replacing the relative clauses printed in **bold** with their shortest possible forms.*

1. The people **who are climbing the tower** are trying to get a better view.

   ....The people climbing the tower are trying to get a better view.....

2. The woman **who is talking to your mother** is my teacher.

   ....

3. The first speed boat **which I ever saw** belonged to my Uncle.

   ....

4. The new battery of the phone **which I had bought at the market** unfortunately didn't last long.

   ....

5. The bouquet was made from flowers **which were grown locally**.

   ....

6. This is the book **which I was talking to you about**.

   ....

18 Adverbial clauses

Adverbial clauses

> **TIP**
> • Prime Time Transition 5: Unit 8 → S. 110

1 Sentence halves

a) Match the sentence halves to form meaningful sentences and copy them into your notebook. Underline the conjunctions in each sentence.

1.	While you were out,	D	A	give me a call on my mobile.
2.	She talked so slowly		B	they couldn't arrest her.
3.	As soon as you have finished collecting the evidence,		C	because the evidence was overwhelming.
4.	Although the police knew she had committed the crime		D	a police officer came who wanted to talk to you.
5.	He was found guilty		E	wherever he wanted to go.
6.	I ordered two teams of crime scene investigators		F	so that you can continue with your tests now.
7.	Unless you know anything about the crime		G	as if she were intoxicated.
8.	The police car took him		H	as if his life were dependent on it.
9.	I fixed the microscope		I	as the area is so big.
10.	He ran as fast		J	please go home and let us do our work.

b) Which information do the adverbial clauses above express?
c) Write two more example sentences for each of the four functions (when, where, how, why).

2 Language in use: Find the correct word

You are going to read a newspaper article on an incident at Bowie High School. Some words are missing from the text. Choose the correct answer (A, B, C or D) for each gap (1–10) in the text. Write your answers in the boxes provided. The first one (0) has been done for you.

Bowie police arrested five teens from the area on burglary and vandalism charges in relation to a break-in at Bowie High School, according to a police report. "It looked … **(0)** something was terribly, terribly wrong," 81-year-old Joseph Battuta reports. He had been on his way home from the bingo hall … **(Q1)** he noticed suspicious movements around Bowie High School. … **(Q2)** the bad weather, Battuta moved closer and discovered a group of teenagers grouping around the school's entrance.

Battuta got worried; luckily he hadn't come in contact with violent young people … **(Q3)** that evening. … **(Q4)** he was frightened, he shouted at the teenagers and announced he would call the police. It took him some time to place the call … **(Q5)** Battuta was too excited to get his mobile out of his pocket quickly. But … **(Q6)** he had called the police straight away they couldn't have been at the scene of crime any quicker due to a shortage of staff.

In the meantime, the teenagers acted … **(Q7)** they hadn't noticed anything and continued to vandalise the property. … **(Q8)** the police arrived, the young offenders tried to escape in all directions. But the Detective Superintendent had anticipated that and had called for backup … **(Q9)** there were enough officers to arrest the vandals. Police found that … **(Q10)** the school's elaborate alarm system the teenagers had managed to enter the property via open windows. Once inside, the suspects vandalised the property, damaged equipment and sprayed a fire extinguisher. Five suspects were arrested on the scene and charged with burglary and vandalism.

112

Adverbial clauses | 18

0	A	only if	B	as if	C	even if	D	so that
Q1	A	like	B	as	C	unless	D	in case
Q2	A	Even	B	Though	C	In spite of	D	Whereas
Q3	A	until	B	whereas	C	because	D	whereeever
Q4	A	Because	B	Only if	C	Until	D	Although
Q5	A	as though	B	while	C	until	D	since
Q6	A	even if	B	unless	C	only if	D	if
Q7	A	so that	B	as soon as	C	such as	D	as if
Q8	A	Not only	B	Until	C	Although	D	As soon as
Q9	A	as if	B	then	C	so that	D	only if
Q10	A	even though	B	until	C	as if	D	despite

0	Q1	Q2	Q3	Q4	Q5	Q6	Q7	Q8	Q9	Q10
B ✓										

3 Connecting sentences

Try out different conjunctions and adverbial clauses to combine the two sentences.

1. The five-cent coin looks very Canadian. It has a picture of a beaver on it.
   The five-cent coin looks very Canadian since it has a picture of a beaver on it.
   Because the five-cent coin has a picture of a beaver on it, it looks very Canadian.

2. You need proper shoes to go hiking in the Alps. The ground is rough and hard.
   ....
   ....

3. My brother started medical training. He drove a lorry for a living.
   ....
   ....

4. The dolphin lives in the sea. It is not a fish, it's a mammal.
   ....
   ....

5. I enjoyed camping out. I was much younger.
   ....
   ....

6. American football players wear lots of protective clothing. They don't get hurt much.
   ....
   ....

7. I took notes. I was taught to use the new accounting software.
   ....
   ....

8. Jake did the ironing. He also prepared breakfast.
   ....
   ....

Unit 1–23 (Vocabulary) Key

Unit 1 Speaking English • The world speaks English (Key)

1 Language in use: Talking about your own language experience

0: C, Q1: A, Q2: B, Q3: D, Q4: B, Q5: D, Q6: A, Q7: D, Q8: B, Q9: A, Q10: D

2 Countries and languages

1. Flemish (Dutch)/French, 2. Bosnian (Serbo-Croatian), 3. Chinese (Mandarin, Cantonese, …), 4. (Serbo-)Croatian, 5. Czech, 6. Danish, 7. Finnish, 8. Greek, 9. Hungarian, 10. English/Irish (Gaelic), 11. Italian/German, 12. Dutch, 13. Polish, 14. Romanian (Rumanian), 15. Russian, 16. Serbo-Croatian (Serbian), 17. Slovakian, 18. Slovenian, 19. German/Italian/French/Romansh, 20. Turkish

3 Finding synonyms: English study tips

1. improve, 2. goal, 3. ask themselves, 4. at that point, 5. learning diary, 6. priorities, 7. presentation, 8. subtitles, 9. appropriate, 10. made a bit simpler

4 Learning tips: Making suggestions, giving advice

a)–b) Individuelle Schüler/innenantworten

5 Finding the right definitions

1. H, 2. E, 3. F, 4. C, 5. A, 6. G, 7. D, 8. B

Unit 2 It's my life • Identities – what next? (Key)

1 Who am I?

a) angry, cheerful, complicated, friendly, frustrated, hard-working, lazy, outgoing, popular, responsible, self-conscious, sensitive, serious, shy, stressed out, tolerant, uneasy, worried
b) Individuelle Schüler/innenantworten

2 Describing a person

a) **Beispielantwort:** 1. angry – furious, 2. quiet – silent, 3. horrible – terrible, 4. beautiful – pretty, 5. easy-going – relaxed, 6. clever – intelligent, 7. loud – noisy, 8. awesome – great
b)–c) Individuelle Schüler/innenantworten

3 Describing character

a) 1. unambitious, 2. inflexible, 3. unfriendly, 4. unhappy, 5. dishonest, 6. unkind, 7. unlucky, 8. unpleasant, 9. impolite, 10. unpunctual, 11. unreliable, 12. insensitive

b) 1. punctual, 2. unreliable, 3. flexible, 4. insensitive, 5. ambitious, 6. unhappy
c) Individuelle Schüler/innenantworten

4 Language in use: What are the qualities a good student should have?

a) 0: L, Q1: G, Q2: J, Q3: D, Q4: I, Q5: A, Q6: F, Q7: H, Q8: E, Q9: K; **Not used:** amusing (B), funny (C)
b) Individuelle Schüler/innenantworten

Unit 3 Up and away (Key)

1 Vocabulary revision

a) **Tickets:** first class, single ticket; **Roads:** motorway; **Rail traffic:** tram; **Road traffic:** bicycle, coach; **Water traffic:** boat, ferry, ocean liner; **Air traffic:** helicopter; **At the airport:** gate; **People:** driver, passenger, pilot; **Places:** bus stop; **Stations:** platform; **Places to book:** tourist office
b)–c) Individuelle Schüler/innenantworten

2 Vocabulary definitions

1. caravan, 2. check-in, 3. ferry, 4. return ticket, 5. coach, 6. gate

3 Talking about a holiday trip

a) 1. of my trip to San Francisco. 2. a ferryboat taking tourists from Alcatraz, the prison island in the Bay, back to San Francisco. 3. visitors to the island like us. 4. the spectacular skyline of the city of San Francisco. 5. fantastic, just a slight breeze on the Bay but sunshine all the way. 6. warm, just the right sort of weather to make a little trip. 7. my wonderful stay in the US last year. 8. I could go back this year. 9. that brought America to life for me.
b) holiday, stay, trip
c) great, terrific, fantastic, wonderful, to bring to life, spectacular, just the right sort of
d) frightening, real horror, to be scared, nightmare, darkest place, to scare, to be scared to death

4 A restaurant review: Putting the record right

Beispielantwort
What can I say about this **excellent** restaurant? It is **simply the best** restaurant in town. They serve traditional food and it tastes **delicious**, the service is **professional** and the location **is gorgeous**. In addition, it is **quite reasonable** and you **get more than what you pay for**. The menu **is large and varied**, certainly something for people who love **superb traditional** dishes. I have been there with friends and family, and **everybody** was happy about it. **I really**

114

enjoyed lunch and evening meals at the restaurant, and **have never been disappointed**. It has always been an **excellent** dining experience as the staff **is characterised by** the personal touch and friendliness one would expect. I **can fully recommend** this place.

5 An emergency call

1, 3, 7, 5, 8, 4, 6, 2
Operator: Fire service. Can you please give me the address where the fire is?
Caroline: 21 Swainstone Road in Maidstone.
Operator: 21 Swainstone Road, Maidstone. Thank you. Is it a house?
Caroline: Yes, it is, a terraced house. The fire's in the upstairs bedroom!
Operator: And are you outside or still in the building?
Caroline: I'm outside, with my little brother.
Operator: Is there anyone else in the building?
Caroline: No, we were the only people in the house. …

Unit 4 Hobbies (Key)

1 Interpreting graphs

a) **1.** graph, **2.** most, **3.** More, **4.** almost/nearly, **5.** surprised, **6.** said/answered, **7.** sleeping, **8.** cent, **9.** second, **10.** 16, **11.** as, **12.** Less
b)–c) Individuelle Schüler/innenantworten

2 Ball games

a) **1.** basketball, **2.** football, **3.** volleyball, **4.** American football, **5.** tennis, **6.** baseball, **7.** golf, **8.** table tennis
b) **1.** In **basketball** you have to throw the ball and pass it to the other players. You can catch it, but you mustn't kick it. You have to throw the ball into the hoop.
2. In **football** you have to kick the ball and pass it to the other players. You can head it, but you mustn't catch it unless you are the goalkeeper.
3. In **volleyball** you have to hit the ball and pass it to the other players. You can head it, but you mustn't catch it.
4. In **tennis** you have to hit the ball and pass it to the other player(s). You can't throw it, head it or kick it.

3 Sports words

a) **Sport:** football, golf, swimming
Place: circuit, court, pitch, pool, rink
Equipment: clubs, crash helmet, net, puck, racket, skates, sticks, trainers, whistle
b) Individuelle Schüler/innenantworten

4 Language in use: My volunteer experiences

0: the, **00:** at, **000:** ✓, **Q1:** if, **Q2:** on, **Q3:** ✓, **Q4:** not, **Q5:** ✓, **Q6:** did, **Q7:** after, **Q8:** ✓, **Q9:** this, **Q10:** from, **Q11:** over, **Q12:** ✓, **Q13:** when, **Q14:** by, **Q15:** ✓, **Q16:** over, **Q17:** at, **Q18:** ✓

5 Volunteering vocabulary

1. donate, **2.** needy, **3.** shelters, **4.** soup, **5.** charity, **6.** Corps

Unit 5 Fifteen minutes of fame • Media-mad

1 On TV

a) **Documentaries:** Antiques Roadshow, Country Show Cook Off, Breadline Britain: Tonight, Easter Eggs Live, James May's Man Lab, The Martin Lewis Money Show, Secret Eaters
Quiz shows: Pointless, The Chase, Eggheads
Game shows: Come Dine with Me, Great British Menu, MasterChef
Drama series: Hollyoaks, EastEnders, Emmerdale (2x)
Current affairs programmes: BBC News, ITV News London, BBC London News, ITV News and Weather, The One Show, Channel 4 News
b) Individuelle Schüler/innenantworten

2 TV vocabulary

a) **1.** coverage; **2.** forecast; **3.** remote control, channel; **4.** soap opera; **5.** breaking; **6.** quiz show; **7.** prime time; **8.** host; **9.** rerun; **10.** anchors
b) Individuelle Schüler/innenantworten

3 In the movies

a) **1.** F, **2.** E, **3.** B, **4.** A, **5.** G, **6.** H, **7.** J, **8.** C, **9.** L, **10.** D, **11.** I, **12.** K
b) Individuelle Schüler/innenantworten

4 Language in use: Teen television addiction

0: designed, **Q1:** addictive, **Q2:** producers, **Q3:** problematic, **Q4:** attractive, **Q5:** real, **Q6:** promising, **Q7:** curiosity, **Q8:** growing, **Q9:** fifth, **Q10:** finally, **Q11:** favourite

5 Agree to disagree

1. worried, **2.** afraid/sorry, **3.** think/believe, **4.** opinion, **5.** differently, **6.** convinced/sure

Unit 6 Music (Key)

1 Vocabulary revision: Music production

Producing your own music: edit music, singing to music, listen to music, edit out, master, record a track, mix, present, work with equipment, pick up sounds, release a song, offer music, make a video, put on the web, publish, make music
Equipment needed: multi-track audio recorder, sound equipment, radio, home computer, studio, microphone, internet connection, software, audio workstation
Songs: tune, vocal track, recording, sound, noise, audio track, raw file, raw data, sound effect, samples, lyrics, melody, poetic texts

2 Language in use: The history of sound recording

0: G, **Q1:** J, **Q2:** C, **Q3:** L, **Q4:** A, **Q5:** I, **Q6:** B, **Q7:** F, **Q8:** D, **Q9:** E;
Not used: singer (H), tape (K)

3 Discussing a song

1. soft, 2. modern, 3. monotonous, 4. melodious, 5. fast,
6. simple, 7. slow, 8. exciting, 9. aggressive, 10. loud

4 File sharing: Is it worth the trouble?

a)–b) Individuelle Schüler/innenantworten

Unit 7 Jobs (Key)

1 Different jobs for different people

a) 1. university lecturer, 2. architect, 3. lawyer, 4. engineer, 5. docotor/nurse, 6. stockbroker, 7. vet, 8. carpenter, 9. plumber, 10. firefighter
b) Individuelle Schüler/innenantworten
c) **Beispielantwort:** 1. lawyer, 2. mechanic, 3. nurse, 4. dentist, 5. doctor, 6. police officer, 7. vet, 8. sales manager, 9. bricklayer, 10. soldier

2 Moving up the career ladder

a) **1:** D, **2:** F, **3:** A, **4:** G, **5:** B, **6:** I, **7:** J, **8:** E, **9:** M, **10:** C, **11:** N, **12:** K, **13:** H, **14:** L
b) **0:** B, **Q1:** G, **Q2:** I, **Q3:** F, **Q4:** C, **Q5:** A, **Q6:** E, **Q7:** K, **Q8:** H, **Q9:** J; **Not used:** customer service (D), working hours (L)

3 Crossword puzzle

a) **Across:** 1. fisherman, 2. miner, 7. artist, 8. programmer, 9. nurse, 10. dentist, 13. astronaut, 15. vet, 18. construction worker, 20. chef, 22. soldier, 23. reporter, 24. athlete
Down: 1. firefighter, 2. musician, 3. doctor, 4. police officer, 5. plumber, 6. scientist, 11. janitor, 12. actor, 14. truck driver, 16. mechanic, 17. singer, 19. pilot, 21. waiter
b) actress, waitress

Unit 8 Crime and suspense (Key)

1 Word search: Crime

a) →: kidnapping (Z. 2, S. 3)¹, shoplifting (Z. 3, S. 1), bribery (Z. 6, S. 2), burglary (Z. 10, S. 4), vandalisam (Z. 11, S. 3), smuggle (Z. 12, S. 4)
←: theft (Z. 1, S. 5), hooliganism (Z. 5, S. 12), crime (Z. 7, S. 5), mugging (Z. 8, S. 8), murder (Z. 9, S. 7)
↓: rape (Z. 9, S. 2), blackmail (Z. 4, S. 9), robbery (Z. 4, S. 11)
↑: offence (Z. 10, S. 1), drug-dealing (Z. 11, S. 6), arson (Z. 8, S. 10), attack (Z. 11, S. 12)

b) 1. theft, 2. robbery, 3. vandalism, 4. drug-dealing, 5. shoplifting, 6. burglary, 7. offence, 8. blackmail, 9. smuggle, 10. murder, 11. hooliganism, 12. arson, 13. bribery, 14. rape, 15. kidnapping, 16. attack, 17. crime, 18. mugging

2 Language in use: Alfred Hitchcock – The Master of Suspense

0: G, **Q1:** L, **Q2:** E, **Q3:** A, **Q4:** M, **Q5:** B, **Q6:** N, **Q7:** D, **Q8:** C, **Q9:** J, **Q10:** F, **Q11:** I; **Not used:** publication (H), shot (K)

3 Finding definitions: Thrillers

1. director, 2. audience, 3. scene, 4. producer, 5. feature film, 6. viewer, 7. thriller, 8. end, 9. background, 10. film industry, 11. masterpiece, 12. mystery, 13. part, 14. suspense, 15. plot, 16. career

4 Language in use: A crime story by Patricia Highsmith

0: ✓, **00:** to, **000:** ✓, **Q1:** attack, **Q2:** ✓, **Q3:** ✓, **Q4:** lonely, **Q5:** ✓, **Q6:** out, **Q7:** lately, **Q8:** strong, **Q9:** ✓, **Q10:** away, **Q11:** to, **Q12:** ✓, **Q13:** ✓, **Q14:** very, **Q15:** working, **Q16:** her, **Q17:** ✓

Unit 9 Australia (Key)

1 Language in use: The Great Barrier Reef

0: C, **Q1:** B, **Q2:** C, **Q3:** A, **Q4:** D, **Q5:** B, **Q6:** D, **Q7:** A, **Q8:** B, **Q9:** A, **Q10:** D

2 Vocabulary revision: Angela

1. G, 2. I, 3. F, 4. L, 5. J, 6. E, 7. D, 8. B, 9. K, 10. A, 11. C, 12. H

3 Linking sentences with who or which/that

1. girl who comes, 2. friends who are, 3. Angela who is, 4. a jewellery store which/that was, 5. bad mood which/that had, 6. the shop manager who told

4 Linking sentences with and, but or because

1. because, 2. but, 3. and

5 Word formation: Prefixes

a) Individuelle Schüler/innenantworten
b) 1. outdated, 2. unchanged, 3. rebuilt, 4. display, 5. overrated, 6. recharge, 7. unborn, 8. mislaid, 9. undated, 10. misspelled, 11. misled

---

¹ Der erste Buchstabe des gesuchten Wortes befindet sich in Zeile 2, Spalte 3. Dieses System wird auf alle Wörter angewandt, egal in welche Richtung sie zu lesen sind.

Unit 10 Books (Key)

1 Positive, negative or both?

Positive: amazing, astonishing, authentic, award-winning, believable, bestselling, clever, extraordinary, fascinating, funny, hilarious, honest, impressive, incredible, inspirational, magical, memorable, moving, original, refreshing, spectacular, thrilling, touching, unique, well-written
Negative: boring, disturbing, far-fetched, frightening, predictable, shocking, stereotypical, weak
Both: exciting, fast-paced, heart-breaking, monumental, realistic, revealing, slow-moving, thought-provoking

2 Sentence builder

Beispielantwort
1. The talented author recently published the new part of the Vampire hit series *The last bite*.
2. The well-written blurb made me really interested in the book and so I bought it.
3. In the heart-breaking final chapter the hero finally married his love and they lived happily ever after.
4. The realistic characters make this book memorable and thought-provoking.
5. The original cover showing a picture of Picasso usually grabs everybody's attention.
6. The fast-paced ending was so exciting that it kept me sleepless for days.
7. The informative introduction is necessary to understand the rather complicated plot.
8. The thrilling plot makes this book a real page-turner. I finished it within two days.
9. The award-winning publishing house has been in business for more than thirty years.
10. The honest review reveals the positive and the negative sides of the book.
11. The spectacular setting of the romance is described in great detail.
12. The hilarious story made me laugh out many times.

3 Word search: Books

a) →: fable (Z. 1, S. 3), handbook (Z. 5, S. 7)
  ←: dictionary (Z. 2, S. 15), horror (Z. 15, S. 14)
  ↓: poem (Z. 1, S. 10), fantasy (Z. 5, S. 15)
  ↑: adventure (Z. 9, S. 16), novel (Z. 5, S. 17)
  ↘: mystery (Z. 5, S. 1), diary (Z. 6, S. 8)
  ↖: speech (Z. 9, S. 7), biography (Z. 9, S. 9)
  ↙: romance (Z. 4, S. 13)
  ↗: thriller (Z. 10, S. 1), drama (Z. 12, S. 1)
b) **1.** biography, **2.** poems, **3.** thrillers, **4.** dictionary, **5.** fable, **6.** speeches, **7.** handbook, **8.** diary, **9.** Horror/Mystery, **10.** fantasy/mystery

4 Language in use: Book review of *Twilight* by Stephenie Meyer

0: loved, **Q1:** possible, **Q2:** stereotypical, **Q3:** beautiful, **Q4:** mysterious, **Q5:** fascinating, **Q6:** written, **Q7:** actually, **Q8:** wonderful, **Q9:** character, **Q10:** sweetest

Unit 11 Politics (Key)

1 Word search: Politics

a) →: voter (Z. 11, S. 2)
  ←: prime (Z. 1, S. 6)
  ↓: rule (Z. 2, S. 2), party (Z. 6, S. 8), commons (Z. 4, S. 10)
  ↑: polling (Z. 7, S. 1), queen (Z. 11, S. 7), elections (Z. 11, S. 9), candidate (Z. 9, S. 11)
  ↙: majority (Z. 1, S. 8), president (Z. 1, S. 9)
  ↗: member (Z. 6, S. 2), government (Z. 10, S. 1), congress (Z. 11, S. 1), senate (Z. 10, S. 3)
b) **1.** candidate, **2.** commons, **3.** congress, **4.** elections, **5.** government, **6.** majority, **7.** member, **8.** party, **9.** polling, **10.** president, **11.** prime, **12.** queen, **13.** rule, **14.** senate, **15.** voter

2 Language in use: The American Revolution

0: D, **Q1:** L, **Q2:** E, **Q3:** I, **Q4:** A, **Q5:** H, **Q6:** K, **Q7:** B, **Q8:** J, **Q9:** F, **Q10:** C, **Q11:** G; **Not used:** take in (M), territories (N)

3 Research: The fathers of the American Revolution

1. George Washington, **2.** Thomas Jefferson

Unit 12 Strange realities (Key)

1 Language in use: A strange story

0: artist, **Q1:** careful, **Q2:** painful, **Q3:** disappearance, **Q4:** Nearly, **Q5:** illness, **Q6:** Happiness, **Q7:** desperately, **Q8:** dangerous, **Q9:** Suddenly, **Q10:** impossible, **Q11:** Confused

2 Linking words: Time and sequence

First beat together butter and sugar in a large bowl.
While you are beating in the eggs and vanilla extract, add a few drops of food colouring to the mixture.
Stir the flour into the butter mixture **before** you work it into a dough using floured hands.
After having divided the dough into two portions, leave it to chill in the fridge for one hour.
While preheating the oven to 170 °C, line two baking trays with baking paper.
After having rolled the dough out on a lightly floured work surface, cut shapes out with the Halloween cutters.
While you are placing the cookies onto the baking tray, leave a gap between them.
Bake the cookies for 12–15 minutes. **After that**, leave them on the tray for 10 minutes.
When the cookies have cooled off, let your imagination run wild and decorate them.
Finally serve the cookies to your guests who "trick or treat".

3 Linking words: Addition and contrast

a) **Addition:** also, and, as well, in addition, too, what's more
Contrast: although, but, despite, despite the fact that, however, in spite of, though, whereas

b) **1.** Despite, too; **2.** What's more, and; **3.** whereas/but, Despite/In spite of; **4.** though, What's more; **5.** In addition, as well; **6.** despite/in spite of, however

Unit 13 Human rights (Key)

1 Language in use: Amnesty International

0: H, **Q1:** N, **Q2:** G, **Q3:** F, **Q4:** L, **Q5:** B, **Q6:** J, **Q7:** A, **Q8:** K, **Q9:** M, **Q10:** D, **Q11:** C; **Not used:** cut (E), physical (I)

2 Improving your word power

1. violate, **2.** tolerate, **3.** torture, **4.** employer, **5.** slave, **6.** discriminate against, **7.** privacy, **8.** judge

3 A modern heroine

b) **1.** famous, **2.** to campaign, **3.** education, **4.** to ban, **5.** to document, **6.** media, **7.** nominated for

4 Research modern heroes

Individuelle Schüler/innenantworten

Unit 14 Growing up (Key)

1 Who's who?

a) **1.** brother-in-law, **2.** nephew, **3.** cousins, **4.** niece, **5.** grandfather/-dad, **6.** stepfather/-dad, **7.** uncle, **8.** widow, **9.** granddaughter, **10.** stepson

b) Individuelle Schüler/innenantworten

2 A life story

1. Simon was born in Wales in 1975.
2. When he was two years old, his mother got a new job and so he grew up in Switzerland.
3. At the age of 19 Simon went to university, where he met Alexa.
4. He went out with her for two years, but they had lots of arguments, so they eventually split up.
5. In his mid-twenties, Simon met Rebecca.
6. They fell in love and got married in Wales within six months.
7. One year later, Rebecca got pregnant and gave birth to a boy named Jason.
8. But they had a lot of problems in their marriage, so Simon left and they got divorced.
9. Four years later, Rebecca remarried and got her second child, a girl called Leyla.
10. Simon now lives as a single, but he visits Jason and Leyla regularly.

3 How would you describe your best friend?

a) **1.** ambitious – determined, **2.** cheerful – happy, **3.** easy-going – relaxed, **4.** generous – big-hearted, **5.** impatient – nervous, **6.** moody – emotional, **7.** optimistic – confident, **8.** sensitive – compassionate, **9.** sociable – outgoing, **10.** trustworthy – reliable

b) **1.** trustworthy, reliable; **2.** generous, big-hearted; **3.** ambitious, determined; **4.** cheerful, happy; **5.** sensitive, compassionate; **6.** moody, emotional; **7.** easy-going, relaxed; **8.** sociable, outgoing; **9.** optimistic, confident; **10.** impatient, nervous

c)–d) Individuelle Schüler/innenantworten

4 Language in use: Are teenagers the problem?

0: A, **Q1:** C, **Q2:** B, **Q3:** A, **Q4:** D, **Q5:** B, **Q6:** D, **Q7:** A, **Q8:** C, **Q9:** A, **Q10:** D

Unit 15 Multi-ethnic Britain (Key)

1 Finding useful expressions: Multi-ethnic Britain

Beispielantwort

Afro Caribbean, Asian food, Asian restaurants, Black African, Black History Month, British colonies, British economy, British Empire, British population, business people, childhood memories, Chinese take-away, cultural influence, Eastern Europe, economic, economic reasons, ethnic background, ethnic group, ethnic minority, fastest growing, foreign origin, front room, immigration controls, Indian cuisine, mixed race, physical abuse, physical appearance, plantation owners, post-war nation, self-help organisation, slave trade, trade unionists

2 Finding synonyms: Multi-ethnic Britain

1. descend from, **2.** plantation, **3.** population, **4.** statistics, **5.** relationship, **6.** rent, **7.** low wages, **8.** not confined

3 Linking sentence halves

1. G, **2.** K, **3.** A, **4.** I, **5.** C, **6.** F, **7.** B, **8.** D, **9.** E, **10.** H, **11.** J

4 Language in use: What is ethnic food?

0: ✓, **00:** to, **000:** ✓, **Q1:** to, **Q2:** powder, **Q3:** health, **Q4:** mountains, **Q5:** ✓, **Q6:** Then, **Q7:** ✓, **Q8:** stores, **Q9:** and, **Q10:** shock, **Q11:** ✓, **Q12:** not, **Q13:** ✓, **Q14:** their, **Q15:** to, **Q16:** ✓, **Q17:** ✓, **Q18:** not

5 Reading: An interview with Fatima Cummins

11, 5, 9, 2, 8, 6, 12, 3, 7, 4, 10, 1

Unit 16 The Blue Planet (Key)

1 Vocabulary: Environment

a) **Normal phenomena in nature:** carbon dioxide, climate, drought, earthquake, flood, forest fire, nuclear energy, ozone layer, rainforest, typhoon, volcanic eruption, wildlife

Things that may harm the environment: acid rain, climate change, deforestation, desertification, disposable products, endangered species, exhaust fumes, extinction, fertilisers, global warming, greenhouse effect, nuclear waste, pesticides, pollution, unleaded petrol, waste

Things that are good for the environment: animal welfare, conservation, pressure group, recycling, renewable energy, solar energy

b) **1.** climate, **2.** ozone layer, **3.** global warming, **4.** unleaded petrol, **5.** disposable products, **6.** endangered species, **7.** Deforestation, **8.** pressure group, **9.** Animal Welfare, **10.** exhaust fumes

2 Units of measurement

b) **1.** 1.57, **2.** 54.9, **3.** 0.28, **4.** 13.3, **5.** 5, **6.** 11, **7.** 12, **8.** 8.4, **9.** 53.6
c) Individuelle Schüler/innenantworten
d) **1.** 15 miles = 24.135 km, **2.** 3 gallons = 13.64 l, **3.** 107 °F = 41.67 °C, **4.** 10 pints = 5.68 l, **5.** 4 feet = 1.22 m, **6.** 21-inch = 53.34-cm, **7.** 20 miles = 32.18 km, **8.** 88 °F = 31.11 °C

3 Language in use: Global warming causes fish to shrink

a) **0:** L, **Q1:** F, **Q2:** M, **Q3:** D, **Q4:** K, **Q5:** J, **Q6:** A, **Q7:** C, **Q8:** H, **Q9:** G, **Q10:** B, **Q11:** I; **Not used:** migrate (E), tropics (N)
b) **1.** D, **2.** F, **3.** B, **4.** E, **5.** G, **6.** C, **7.** H, **8.** A

Unit 17 Making a difference (Key)

1 Finding synonyms and opposites

Synonyms: 1. rich; **2.** to say no; **3.** to discover; **4.** to collect money; **5.** aggressive; **6.** prejudiced, unfair, partial; **7.** to help; **8.** sure of oneself
Opposites: 1. poor; **2.** to agree; **3.** to lose; **4.** to spend money; **5.** non-violent, friendly, peaceful; **6.** unbiased/tolerant; **7.** to abandon; **8.** insecure/timid

2 Ways to evaluate

Positive: beneficial, correct, encouraging, fair, helpful, just, loyal, practical, reasonable, responsible, right, true
Negative: detrimental, disappointing, disloyal, frustrating, incorrect, irresponsible, not right, unfair, unjust, unpractical, untrue, wrong

3 Language in use: Make a Difference Day

0: C, **Q1:** B, **Q2:** C, **Q3:** A, **Q4:** D, **Q5:** C, **Q6:** D, **Q7:** A, **Q8:** B, **Q9:** B, **Q10:** D

4 Finding reasons why people may have problems

Beispielantwort
1. **problems in the job:** losing your job, becoming unemployed, not being able to work in an organised way, working at a slow pace, not being able to work in adverse conditions, being sacked, being laid off, not being able to do complex jobs, being made redundant, being inflexible
2. **problems in the family:** having to care for sick or old relatives, having to care for close relatives, being separated from one's family, going through a divorce, running away from home, violence in the family
3. **problems with housing:** being unable to afford heating, not being able to move to another place, not being able to pay back the mortgage
4. **problems with money:** not being able to pay the rent, having spent too much money, not being able to pay for loans, divorce settlements
5. **mental problems:** losing concentration, not being able to stand pressure, not being able to cope with stress, not being able to do regular work
6. **physical problems:** not being able to do hard physical work, not being able to lift heavy loads

Unit 18 Globalisation (Key)

1 Globalisation shakes the world

a) **Z. 68:** billing, **Z. 78:** economic growth, **Z. 27:** economic superpower, **Z. 17:** from boom to bust, **Z. 25:** industrial revolution, **Z. 33:** information technology, **Z. 7:** to lay off sb., **Z. 40:** multinational company, **Z. 46:** outsourcing, **Z. 43:** overseas, **Z. 67:** payroll, **Z. 38:** post-war years, **Z. 55:** services sector, **Z. 22:** trade, **Z. 73:** white collar job
b) **1.** O, **2.** F, **3.** B, **4.** M, **5.** I, **6.** N, **7.** H, **8.** J, **9.** E, **10.** G, **11.** D, **12.** C, **13.** K, **14.** A, **15.** L
c) Individuelle Schüler/innenantworten

2 Language in use: Outsourcing the news

0: of, **00:** line, **000:** ✓, **Q1:** at, **Q2:** ✓, **Q3:** over, **Q4:** are, **Q5:** balance, **Q6:** ✓, **Q7:** of, **Q8:** pretty, **Q9:** all, **Q10:** ✓, **Q11:** though, **Q12:** is, **Q13:** whole, **Q14:** ✓, **Q15:** mistakably, **Q16:** ✓, **Q17:** ✓

3 Outsourcing vocabulary

1. external, **2.** outsourcing, **3.** activities, **4.** talent, **5.** staffing, **6.** lowering, **7.** developing, **8.** compete, **9.** quality, **10.** unemployed

Unit 19 South Africa (Key)

1 Find the right meaning

1. C, **2.** F, **3.** D, **4.** A, **5.** G, **6.** H, **7.** B, **8.** E

2 The History of the African National Congress

In 1912 the African National Congress was formed to bring all Africans together as one people. In 1944 Nelson

Mandela joined the ANC. In the 1950s mass resistance to Apartheid started. In 1960 the ANC was banned. In 1961 the armed struggle against the government began. From 1964 to 1990 Nelson Mandela was in prison for anti-Apartheid activism. In 1990 the ban against the ANC was lifted. In 1994 the ANC won in the first free South African elections with 62.6% of the votes. In 1994 Nelson Mandela was elected as the first black president of South Africa. In the years 1999, 2004 and 2009 the ANC won three elections in a row.

3 Language in use: *Cry freedom*

a) 0: E, **Q1:** J, **Q2:** I, **Q3:** G, **Q4:** H, **Q5:** L, **Q6:** F, **Q7:** C, **Q8:** A, **Q9:** B; **Not used:** between (D), under (K)

b) **1.** troubled, **2.** to arrest, **3.** radical, **4.** view, **5.** to stop sb. from doing sth., **6.** originally, **7.** to monitor, **8.** to flee, **9.** to campaign

4 Language in use: Holidays

0: Travelling, **Q1:** rest, **Q2:** internet (facilities/access), **Q3:** en-suite, **Q4:** laundry, **Q5:** facilities, **Q6:** hidden/quiet/secluded, **Q7:** parking, **Q8:** family

5 Word search: Kruger National Park

➔: lodge (Z. 1, S. 1), camp (Z. 1, S. 11), chalet (Z. 5, S. 1), tours (Z. 8, S. 1), safari (Z. 9, S. 5), vegetation (Z. 12, S. 3)
⬅: bushman (Z. 2, S. 7), wildlife (Z. 2, S. 15), tent (Z. 3, S. 6), mammal (Z. 6, S. 6), adventure (Z. 7, S. 11)
⬇: archeology (Z. 2, S. 2), ranger (Z. 8, S. 4), reptile (Z. 1, S. 8), diversity (Z. 5, S. 9), destination (Z. 2, S. 12), fish (Z. 8, S. 14)
⬆: savannah (Z. 10, S. 11), flagship (Z. 8, S. 14)
↖: environmental (Z. 13, S. 13)
↙: protect (Z. 8, S. 10), visitors (Z. 8, S. 11)

Unit 20 The world of work (Key)

1 Working in an office

a) **1.** manufactures, **2.** factory, **3.** types, **4.** customers, **5.** invoices, **6.** paperwork, **7.** round, **8.** appointments, **9.** arranges, **10.** departments, **11.** agenda, **12.** minutes

b) **1:** D, **2:** E, **3:** A, **4:** H, **5:** M, **6:** J, **7:** C, **8:** G, **9:** N, **10:** L, **11:** F, **12:** I, **13:** K, **14:** B

2 Compound nouns

1. armchair, **2.** blackmail, **3.** Brainstorming, **4.** keyboard, **5.** overtime, **6.** timesheet, **7.** filing cabinet, **8.** notice board, **9.** briefcase, **10.** wastepaper basket

3 Word search: Vocabulary for attending meetings

a) ➔: meet (Z. 9, S. 3), PowerPoint (Z. 12, S. 1), handout (Z. 13, S. 1)
⬅: marker (Z. 8, S. 9), projector (Z. 11, S. 9)
⬇: handshake (Z. 1, S. 11), chairs (Z. 9, S. 13)
⬆: date (Z. 6, S. 9), presentation (Z. 13, S. 12), flipchart (Z. 13, S. 15)
↘: whiteboard (Z. 1, S. 1), OHP (Z. 6, S. 8), tables (Z. 1, S. 15)
↖: diary (Z. 12, S. 20), clipboard (Z. 9, S. 20)
↙: presenter (Z. 7, S. 14), slides (Z. 10, S. 19)
↗: calendar (Z. 8, S. 1), colleagues (Z. 10, S. 1), time (Z. 14, S. 17)

b) **1.** colleagues, **2.** meet, **3.** calendar/diary, **4.** presentation, **5.** data projector, **6.** slides, **7.** flipchart/whiteboard, **8.** handout

4 Language in use: Tips to boost your interview skills

0: prepare, **Q1:** impression, **Q2:** handshake, **Q3:** wear, **Q4:** code, **Q5:** said, **Q6:** interest, **Q7:** find, **Q8:** information

Unit 21 Famous speeches (Key)

1 Word formation

Verb: dominate, compete, protest, struggle, grow, talk, succeed
Noun (thing): freedom, competition, struggle, talk, success
Noun (person): freedom fighter, dominator, protester, talker
Adjective: free, dominant, competitive, growing

2 Language in use: Martin Luther King, Jr.

0: ✓, **00:** to, **000:** ✓, **Q1:** always, **Q2:** ✓, **Q3:** the, **Q4:** ✓, **Q5:** ✓, **Q6:** ever, **Q7:** ✓, **Q8:** it, **Q9:** the, **Q10:** and, **Q11:** doing, **Q12:** ✓, **Q13:** numbers, **Q14:** then, **Q15:** ✓, **Q16:** year, **Q17:** ✓, **Q18:** was, **Q19:** ✓, **Q20:** for

3 Working with synonyms

a) **1.** C, **2.** A, **3.** E, **4.** B, **5.** G, **6.** J, **7.** K, **8.** D, **9.** F, **10.** H, **11.** I

b) **1.** to be engaged in → are engaged in, **2.** to be rooted in → is … rooted in, **3.** to dedicate to → dedicated, **4.** to emerge → emerged, **5.** to exploit → are exploiting, **6.** to make sacrifices → made … sacrifices, **7.** to persuade sb. → persuade, **8.** to postpone → postpone, **9.** to resemble → resemble, **10.** to surrender → surrender, **11.** to underestimate → underestimate

4 Commenting on a speech

a)–b) Individuelle Schüler/innenantworten

Unit 22 Sports (Key)

1 *Do, play* or *go*?

1. go, **2.** playing, **3.** has been doing, **4.** went, **5.** plays, **6.** goes, **7.** play, **8.** doing, **9.** go, **10.** does

2 Equipment, scoring and venues

1. **American Football:** ball, cleats, protective pads – down, half, point, quarter, yard – field
2. **Athletics:** cleats – metre, yard – track
3. **Baseball:** ball, bat, glove, protective pads – inning, out, point – field
4. **Chess:** board, piece – game, move – board
5. **Football:** ball, cleats, net – half, metre, point – pitch
6. **Golf:** ball, clubs – strokes – course
7. **Ice hockey:** net, protective pads, puck, stick – game, half, point, quarter – rink
8. **Squash:** ball, racket – game, point – court
9. **Swimming:** suit – length, metre – pool
10. **Table tennis:** ball, net, paddle – game, point – table
11. **Tennis:** ball, racket – game, match, point, set – court
12. **Volleyball:** ball, net – game, point – court

3 Extreme sports

a) Individuelle Schüler/innenantworten mit den folgenden (Extrem-)Sportarten: **1.** bungee jumping, **2.** hang gliding, **3.** in-line skating, **4.** marathon running, **5.** mountain biking, **6.** rock climbing, **7.** scuba diving, **8.** sky diving, **9.** snow boarding, **10.** water skiing

b) **1.** bungee jump, **2.** rock climbing, **3.** Scuba diving, **4.** marathon, **5.** hang glider, **6.** mountain bike, **7.** snow boarding, **8.** inline skate, **9.** sky diving, **10.** water skiers

4 Language in use: From the playing field to the laboratory

0: lose, **Q1:** wonder, **Q2:** taking/using, **Q3:** affect/damage/destroy, **Q4:** dependent, **Q5:** countries, **Q6:** enhance/improve, **Q7:** test, **Q8:** pass, **Q9:** wrong, **Q10:** allowing/legalising/permitting, **Q11:** athletes/those

Unit 23 Beauty and fashion trends (Key)

1 Vocabulary: Words beginning with *com-* and *con-*

1. I, **2.** G, **3.** O, **4.** M, **5.** C, **6.** J, **7.** F, **8.** L, **9.** A, **10.** H, **11.** D, **12.** B, **13.** R, **14.** P, **15.** S, **16.** Q, **17.** N, **18.** K, **19.** E

2 Word search: Adjectives to describe fashion

↓: **1.** startling (Z. 3, S. 1), **2.** awesome (Z. 2, S. 2), **3.** spectacular (Z. 1, S. 3), **4.** phenomenal (Z. 1, S. 4), **5.** strange (Z. 1, S. 5), **6.** amazing (Z. 1, S. 6), **7.** inspiring (Z. 3, S. 7), **8.** shocking (Z. 4, S. 8), **9.** ridiculous (Z. 2, S. 9), **10.** stunning (Z. 2, S. 10), **11.** great (Z. 5, S. 11)
→: astonishing (Z. 5, S. 1)

3 Language in use: Beauty pageants

0: C, **Q1:** B, **Q2:** A, **Q3:** B, **Q4:** D, **Q5:** B, **Q6:** C, **Q7:** C, **Q8:** A, **Q9:** D, **Q10:** C

4 Language in use: My kind of style

0: B, **Q1:** C, **Q2:** E, **Q3:** H, **Q4:** D, **Q5:** M, **Q6:** N, **Q7:** J, **Q8:** K, **Q9:** L, **Q10:** G, **Q11:** A; **Not used:** in spite of (F), moreover (I)

5 Commenting on fashion issues

1. good, **2.** well, **3.** wide, **4.** widely, **5.** greatly, **6.** great, **7.** fantastic, **8.** well

Unit 1–18 (Grammar) Key

Unit 1 Present forms (Key)

1 Present tense simple: Bilingual upbringing

have – want – means – grow up – report – have – can – remember – get – is – have – have – do not know

2 Present tense progressive: Mini dialogues 1

1. Mum: What <u>are</u> you <u>doing</u> in the bathroom? Come on or you'll be late.
   Lucas: I'<u>m</u> not <u>doing</u> anything. I <u>am</u> just <u>getting</u> ready, that's all.
2. Karen: Why <u>are</u> you <u>pushing</u> me all the time? Don't you see that I'<u>m</u> <u>talking</u> on the phone?
   Greg: Sorry, Karen.
3. Sue: Look at her. She <u>is</u> just <u>ignoring</u> me.
   Leah: Come on, she <u>is</u> just <u>talking</u> to the new boy from year 6. She has got a crush on him.

3 Choose the correct simple or progressive form

1. spend, **2.** is staying, **3.** lives, **4.** is visiting, **5.** wants, **6.** likes, **7.** goes, **8.** don't think, **9.** am not feeling, **10.** does not mind

4 Questions and answers

1. Do you like it when people talk on their mobiles on the bus?
2. Which languages do you learn at school?
3. What are you working on at the moment?
4. Who do you talk to normally?

5 Negations in the present tense: Mini dialogues 2

1. am not, **2.** don't, **3.** isn't, **4.** doesn't

121

6 Fill in the correct simple or progressive form

1. read, **2.** work, **3.** are coming, **4.** help, **5.** knows, **6.** have, **7.** are singing

Unit 2 Past forms (Key)

1 Past simple: Writing a report

a) **1.** flew, **2.** checked in, **3.** went, **4.** had, **5.** listened, **6.** took part, **7.** met, **8.** had, **9.** had, **10.** visited, **11.** had, **12.** went, **13.** took part, **14.** listened, **15.** flew
b) Individuelle Schüler/innenantworten

2 Past simple vs. past progressive 1: A mysterious story

a) **1.** lost, **2.** was running, **3.** was going, **4.** found, **5.** was trying, **6.** appeared, **7.** was watching, **8.** rang, **9.** dropped, **10.** was ringing, **11.** waited, **12.** stepped, **13.** was smiling, **14.** broke, **15.** went, **16.** was watching, **17.** stopped, **18.** jumped, **19.** ran, **20.** was staring
b)–c) Individuelle Schüler/innenantworten

3 Language in use: Past simple vs. past progressive 2: Inventions

0: I, **Q1:** B, **Q2:** D, **Q3:** G, **Q4:** C, **Q5:** F, **Q6:** J, **Q7:** K, **Q8:** E; **Not used:** ate (A), was melting (H)

4 Past vs. past perfect: The history of a great place

b) **1. After** Sir Francis Drake **had failed** to take possession of the area in 1579, Mission Dolores **was founded** in the 18th century by the Spaniard Fra Junipero Serra.
2. After the Spaniards **had taken** possession of Mexico, they **sailed** north to the Bay Area from Mexico to find new places to settle.
3. The first settlement **had been** originally named Yerba Buena after a local herb **before** the town **was renamed** San Francisco in 1847.
4. San Francisco **had been** a small town of about 1,000 people **before** its population **rose** to 25,000 in 1848–1849.

Unit 3 Present perfect and other past forms (Key)

1 Present perfect simple or progressive 1

Simple: 2, 3, 5
Progressive: 1, 4, 6

2 Present perfect simple or progressive 2

1. has been learning, **2.** have given up, **3.** have … been waiting, **4.** have … had, **5.** has been working, **6.** has not finished, **7.** has uprooted

3 Present perfect with *for* and *since*

a)–b)
1. I have been reading the book <u>for about an hour</u> […].
2. I have been trying to call you <u>for more than an hour</u>.
3. Colin has been working on his new book <u>for about three months</u> now […].
c)–d)
4. Clare has been working on her presentation <u>since 7 p.m.</u>
5. My sister has been learning Croatian <u>since she was two</u>.

4 Duration or point of time?

a) **Duration:** seven hours, two minutes, several years, two months, six weeks
Point of time: yesterday, a week ago, Sunday, Christmas, November 3rd, … I first met her, then
b) Individuelle Schüler/innenantworten

5 Signal words for the past tense and for the present perfect tense

Past tense: a week ago, last week/month/year, yesterday, on September 15th, at Christmas
Present perfect tense: already, ever, just, lately, never, now, recently, since, so far, up to now

6 Present perfect and other past forms 1: Facebooking

1. Have … been, **2.** have been, **3.** did … sign up, **4.** started, **5.** gave, **6.** showed, **7.** was, **8.** have been posting, **9.** did … spend, **10.** checked, **11.** posted, **12.** was, **13.** kept, **14.** shut down, **15.** spent, **16.** did

7 Present perfect and other past forms 2: Complaining

1. have gone, **2.** wanted, **3.** were, **4.** have not been, **5.** has not been repaired, **6.** has contributed, **7.** was, **8.** talked, **9.** refused, **10.** have had

Unit 4 Future forms (Key)

1 A holiday in Italy

a) **1.** will like, **2.** am going, **3.** are visiting, **4.** will let, **5.** does not start, **6.** includes, **7.** arrives, **8.** picks us up, **9.** takes, **10.** will be, **11.** looks, **12.** will have, **13.** leaves, **14.** am seeing, **15.** will do
b) Individuelle Schüler/innenantworten

2 A school project in trouble

1. are going to do, **2.** will probably get, **3.** will come, **4.** will phone, **5.** will have, **6.** are we going to do, **7.** will not be able, **8.** am going to meet, **9.** will all work out

3 Future situations

Beispielantwort
1. I'm sorry, I'll make you another one.
2. I'm meeting my uncle and aunt at the railway station.
3. Which countries are you going to visit?
4. I'm going to be in a play!
5. I'll pay you back as soon as I have received my pocket money.
6. Will you please turn the volume down?

Unit 5 Modal verbs (Key)

1 Did this really happen?

a) 1. may/might/could, 2. can't/are not able to, 3. are not allowed to/mustn't/can't, 4. should, 5. may/might/should, 6. can't, 7. could, 8. shouldn't, 9. must, 10. may/might/can

b) Individuelle Schüler/innenantworten

c) 1. The man may/might/could cause trouble.
2. The employees can't open the safe because they don't know the code.
3. They mustn't open the safe without their boss.
4. The boss may/might/could come back before lunch.
5. The employee shouldn't have said that they could call the robber back.
6. The employees must/need to stay at the back of the shop while the robber is being arrested.

2 Should have, would have, could have

Beispielantwort
must(n't): The robber must put his hands in the air.
need(n't): The employees need to cooperate with the robber so that he doesn't get angry.
should(n't): The shop owner should have installed an alarm system.
(don't) have to: The employees have to call the robber on his mobile phone.
had better (not): The employee had better not said that they could call the robber back.
ought (not) to: They ought not to argue with the robber.

3 Language in use: Working in reality TV

0: I, Q1: D/A, Q2: C, Q3: G, Q4: H, Q5: J, Q6: A/D, Q7: E; **Not used:** may not (B), needn't (F)

4 DOs and DON'Ts in reality TV

Beispielantwort
You **should** be yourself./You **must** be yourself!

Unit 6 Conditional clauses (Key)

1 Zero conditional: General truths

1. want to become – have to start, 2. want to learn – is not enough to play, 3. don't want to catch – don't open the window

2 Zero conditional: Giving advice

1. wants, 2. call, 3. are, 4. have, 5. stay, 6. be

3 Conditional 1: Real conditions

1. If he calls me, I will pretend not to be at home.
2. If they send me e-mails, I will not answer them.
3. If you water the plants too much, they will lose their leaves.
4. If you do not clear the snow in front of the house, somebody will fall and get hurt.

4 Conditional 2: Unreal, but possible conditions

1. If the rain stopped, we would go to the beach.
2. If I lost my keys, I would not be able to get into the house.
3. If her parents had more money to spend, she could come on holiday with us.
4. If his uncle from Sweden did not come to visit them, Paul would come to the cinema with us.

5 Conditional 2: What would happen if I missed the train?

1. were, 2. would be spoiled, 3. missed, 4. would not be able, 5. would not be able, 6. happened, 7. would try, 8. could hear, 9. would get

6 Conditional 3: Unreal conditions in the past

1. had been, 2. would not have missed, 3. had phoned, 4. would have given, 5. had known, 6. would have booked, 7. had been, 8. would have survived, 9. would not have become, 10. had not owned, 11. would not have had

7 Mixed conditionals

1. would have told, 2. went, 3. knew, 4. had looked, 5. would go, 6. don't come, 7. turned, 8. does not win, 9. is

Unit 7 Passive voice (Key)

1 Past participles: A burglary

1. forced, 2. devastated, 3. thrown, 4. ripped, 5. smashed, 6. called, 7. sent, 8. found, 9. caught, 10. published, 11. hurt, 12. informed

2 Passive voice: The basics

1. The only bridge in the village was destroyed by the thunderstorm.
2. The big bedroom window was smashed by the boys.
3. The church was damaged by the earthquake.
4. Dinner will be served by waiters in white dinner jackets.
5. A song by Vampire Weekend was played by the band.

Key

3 Passive voice: Shifting the focus

1. The door was opened and in came the president.
2. The castle was set on fire.
3. Valuable paintings were destroyed in the course of the fire.
4. The furniture of the house could not be saved.
5. Eventually the building was torn down.

4 Passive voice: Modal verbs

1. The lights must switched off before the performance starts.
2. The criminals must be arrested before it is too late.
3. The car should be washed before the guest of honour arrives.
4. The books can be returned to the library on Sunday.
5. The text on the poster will be changed.
6. The front door could not be closed because of the wind.
7. The cover should be removed before changing the battery.

Unit 8 Indirect speech (Key)

1 A Facebook chat

Beispielantwort
11:20: Quite good, actually. I'm still living with my sister and my dad, but I want to move out. My boyfriend has found a flat we can share.
11:22: We just love the place. It has just been renovated. There's just one problem …
11:24: Oh, it's the rent. It's just a lot more than we can spend per month. I used to work part-time for some years, but I'm going to get a new job to earn more money.
11:26: I'm being interviewed tomorrow, so I have to buy some new clothes for the interview.

2 A job interview

a) 1. had been, 2. the previous year, 3. had worked, 4. had been, 5. had been handling, 6. liked, 7. had gone, 8. wanted, 9. seemed, 10. would work, 11. looked, 12. wanted, 13. enabled, 14. had, 15. was, 16. would be
b) Individuelle Schüler/innenantworten

3 Indirect speech and questions

1. Dad asked me where I was going.
2. The headmaster wanted to know what I would do after I had passed my final exams.
3. The man asked the detective how he had known that he had been the last person who had called Annie.
4. My friend Charlaine asked me where I was going to spend the Christmas weekend.
5. David asked the receptionist when he could see Dr Klein.
6. Mum asked me if I had watched the documentary on meteorologists.
7. The tourist guide asked me if I was going to visit the cathedral.
8. Neville asked his colleague if he/she had seen his 64GB memory stick.
9. The clerk asked me if I had an appointment with Ms Silver.
10. Bernard asked his wife why Judith hadn't phoned until then.

4 Indirect speech and commands, requests and suggestions

1. The school nurse advised Julian to have his eyes tested.
2. The police officer ordered the bank robber to hand over his gun immediately.
3. Mrs Marks asked Mr Stern to take care of her dog for a moment.
4. Mrs Emerson suggested giving an award to the best student of the school.
5. Dad offered to take the children to the zoo.
6. The gym teacher encouraged the boys to have a game of football.
7. The park keeper warned Ruth not to sit on the freshly painted bench.
8. Andrew reminded Cilla to post the letter to granddad.
9. The old man told the children to find a better place to practise the drums.

Unit 9 Gerund and infinitives (Key)

1 Gerunds

1. playing, 2. Writing, 3. helping, 4. reading

2 Verbs followed by gerunds only

a) 1. reading, 2. fighting, 3. doing, 4. reading, 5. walking, 6. losing
b) 1. enjoy, 2. give up, 3. mind, 4. Go on, 5. Imagine, 6. risk

3 Adjectives, nouns and phrases followed by gerunds only

1. cleaning, 2. driving, 3. remembering, 4. going, 5. being

4 Gerunds after prepositions

1. looking, 2. learning, 3. looking, 4. giving, 5. waving, 6. reading, 7. going, 8. asking, 9. losing, 10. buying, 11. writing, 12. saying

5 Verbs followed by gerunds or infinitives

b) 1. acting, 2. learning, 3. looking, 4. being, 5. to take, 6. to buy, 7. to come 8. talking

6 Passive gerunds

1. being looked, 2. being taken, 3. being called

Key

7 Using infinitives: Lost at the airport

did not know what to do – where to go – told her when to come – nobody to talk to – no idea who to ask – expected to be welcomed – decided not to come – know how to contact – wanted to get out – did not know which way to go – allowed me to use – the only person to offer – my chance to get in touch – did not know how to get out

8 Using infinitives with *to* after *for* + (pro)noun

1. to talk, **2.** to get, **3.** to stay, **4.** to get

Unit 10 Participle constructions (Key)

1 Using participle constructions to express reason or time

1. Driving, **2.** running, **3.** Having seen, **4.** having been, **5.** pushing, **6.** Realising, **7.** sitting, **8.** coming, **9.** Having been

2 Using present and past participle constructions to link sentences

a) **1.** E, **2.** I, **3.** B, **4.** H, **5.** G, **6.** A, **7.** D, **8.** C, **9.** J, **10.** F
b)
  1. Having witnessed the accident only moments before, Carlo rushed to help the victims.
  2. Known as the Corn State, Iowa is one of the major producers of corn in the US.
  3. Tapping her foot, the shop assistant stared at Fred.
  4. Showing genuine concern, Misha looked at Natasha.
  5. Having been poorly paid for his compositions, the artist died penniless.
  6. Happily, the children danced around their igloo made of hard-packed snow.
  7. Looking for her wallet, Silvie opened her bag.

3 Using relative clauses to replace present and past participle constructions

1. The man who is crossing the road right now is our new neighbour.
2. Motorists who drive under the influence of drugs or alcohol are likely to cause accidents.
3. Freddy, who was already sitting in his car, waved us goodbye.
4. People with children who suffer from leukaemia have a lot of worries.
5. There has just been a terror warning for all planes which fly to Syria this time tomorrow.
6. The Golden Gate Bridge, which was completed in 1937, has become a famous landmark of San Francisco.
7. Anyone who is found guilty of drug possession in Singapore faces the death penalty.

Unit 11 Verbs and their meaning (Key)

1 *Let, make* or *have*

1. I had my fence mended on Friday.
2. I had my dishwasher repaired on Tuesday.
3. Let Jimmy do it! It's his turn.
4. Dad made me clean the car.
5. I had my flat redecorated.
6. Philip's mum made him go shopping.
7. Let her climb up the tree if she wants to.

2 Verbs of perception

1. open, **2.** going, **3.** go, **4.** blowing, **5.** trying, **6.** talking

3 Dynamic and stative verbs: Examples

Dynamic verbs: call, drive, find, read, study, tell, travel
Stative verbs: imagine, know, like, realise, think, understand, want

4 Dynamic and stative verbs: Simple or continuous?

1. was reading, **2.** suddenly realised, **3.** had found, **4.** knew, **5.** wanted, **6.** really liked, **7.** called, **8.** thought, **9.** would like, **10.** did not understand, **11.** imagined, **12.** thought, **13.** told, **14.** wanted, **15.** nearly drove, **16.** understood

Unit 12 Nouns and articles (Key)

1 Plurals of nouns

a) **1.** beliefs, **2.** Dutchmen, **3.** fathers-in-law, **4.** teeth, **5.** flies, **6.** lives, **7.** mice, **8.** formulas/formulae
b) **1.** pieces of music, **2.** litres/bottles/glasses of water, **3.** pieces of information, **4.** slices/pieces/loaves of bread, **5.** bowls/kinds of soup, **6.** sheets of paper, **7.** packets/bars of butter, **8.** pieces of luggage, **9.** cubes/spoons of sugar, **10.** bottles/types of ketchup, **11.** litres/gallons of petrol, **12.** cartons/glasses of milk
c) **1.** pieces of music, **2.** pieces of information, **3.** kinds of soup, **4.** bottles/types of ketchup, **5.** slices/pieces of bread, **6.** litres/bottles/glasses of water, **7.** litres/gallons of petrol, **8.** cubes/spoons of sugar, **9.** pieces of luggage, **10.** packets/bars of butter, **11.** sheets of paper, **12.** cartons of milk

2 Training for a bikeathon: Using articles correctly 1

a) **1.** cereal, **2.** an egg, **3.** a sandwich, **4.** an apple, **5.** celery soup, **6.** a roll, **7.** spaghetti, **8.** tomato sauce, **9.** a chocolate bar
b) Individuelle Schüler/innenantworten

3 Language in use: Using articles correctly 2

0: the, **00:** ✓, **000:** ✓, **Q1:** ✓, **Q2:** a, **Q3:** the, **Q4:** ✓, **Q5:** the, **Q6:** the, **Q7:** a, **Q8:** an, **Q9:** ✓, **Q10:** the, **Q11:** a, **Q12:** the, **Q13:** a, **Q14:** the, **Q15:** ✓, **Q16:** the

Key

Unit 13 Comparison of adjectives (Key)

1 How to form comparisons

a) **Table 1:** easy – easier – easiest, weird – weirder – weirdest, strange – stranger – strangest, few – fewer – fewest, tough – tougher – toughest, small – smaller – smallest, smart – smarter – smartest
Table 2: expensive – more expensive – most expensive, unusual – more unusual – most unusual, famous – more famous – most famous, bizarre – more bizarre – most bizarre, popular – more popular – most popular, fascinating – more fascinating – most fascinating, stylish – more stylish – most stylish, favourite – more favourite – most favourite

b) dead, real, golden

2 Adjectives: Comparisons 1

1. weirdest, **2.** most popular, **3.** most bizarre, **4.** smarter, **5.** most fascinating, **6.** unusual, **7.** most famous, **8.** best, **9.** the most stylish

3 Adjectives: Comparisons 2

1. fewer, **2.** good, **3.** nearest, **4.** next, **5.** latest, **6.** last

4 Adjectives: Comparisons 3

1a. Ben is slower than Jamie.
1b. Jamie is quicker than Ben.
2a. Francis was as good as Sue.
3a. Carl is as young as Sally.
3b. Patricia is older than Carl and Sally.
3c. Sally is not as old as Patricia.
4a. Ian has more money than Paul.
4b. Paul has less money than Ian.
5a. Diana is more reliable than Joan and less reliable than Justine.
5b. Justine is the most reliable.
5c. Joan is less reliable than Diana.

Unit 14 Adjectives and adverbs of manner and degree (Key)

1 News from the music camp

1. safely, **2.** new, **3.** well, **4.** really, **5.** near, **6.** pleasant, **7.** busy, **8.** hard, **9.** surprisingly, **10.** easily, **11.** different, **12.** absolutely, **13.** cheeky

2 Using adverbs correctly

a) **1.** well – good, **2.** nervously – nervous, **3.** hard – hardly, **4.** pretty – prettily, **5.** lately – late
b) Individuelle Schüler/innenantworten

3 Language in use: A musical evening

0: better, **Q1:** brilliantly, **Q2:** easily, **Q3:** hard, **Q4:** fast, **Q5:** accurately, **Q6:** (the) most, **Q7:** confidently, **Q8:** traditionally, **Q9:** slowly, **Q10:** patiently, **Q11:** terribly

4 Position of adverbs

a) **Correct sentences:** 3, 6, 7
Beispielantwort:
1. The police have already been informed about the attempted attack.
2. A new law was passed by Parliament yesterday.
4. If you run faster, you might catch your bus.
5. Since the Norman Conquest Britain has never been invaded.
8. Floods have frequently caused serious damage to the village.

b) 1. We must finish our work today.
2. Children often prefer junk food to healthy meals.
3. Travelling long distances by ship is rarely necessary today.
4. Can the effects of global warming be observed everywhere?
5. The protesters firmly believed in the success of their joint efforts.
6. Our committee meets in the town hall on Tuesday every week.
7. We have hardly got enough petrol to reach the next filling station.
8. The meeting will take place soon.

5 Adjectives and adverbs: Ancient civilisations

1. common, **2.** oldest, **3.** in, **4.** first, **5.** frequently, **6.** well, **7.** highly, **8.** developed, **9.** present-day, **10.** mysteriously, **11.** ago, **12.** extremely, **13.** technologically, **14.** own, **15.** as, **16.** as, **17.** ancient, **18.** more amazing, **19.** human, **20.** used, **21.** mysterious, **22.** hardly, **23.** further

Unit 15 Prepositions and phrasal verbs (Key)

1 Prepositions of place 1

on: on a bus, on a train, on a plane, on a ship, on a bicycle, on a motorbike, on a horse, on the radio, on television, on the way
in: in a taxi, in a helicopter, in a boat, in a lift, in the newspaper, in the sky
at: at school, at university, at college, at the top, at the bottom, at the side

2 Prepositions of place 2

1. in; **2.** in, at; **3.** on; **4.** on; **5.** on; **6.** On; **7.** at; **8.** at; **9.** at; **10.** On

3 Prepositions of place 3

1. at; **2.** in, in, at; **3.** on; **4.** In; **5.** at; **6.** at; **7.** at; **8.** at; **9.** in; **10.** At

4 Prepositions of time

1. at, **2.** at, **3.** in, **4.** on, **5.** At, **6.** at, **7.** On, **8.** from – to, **9.** until, **10.** on, **11.** At, **12.** by, **13.** in, **14.** during, **15.** At, **16.** at, **17.** for, **18.** In, **19.** at, **20.** At, **21.** by, **22.** In

5 Phrasal verbs 1: Prepositions

1. with; **2.** about; **3.** in; **4.** after; **5.** for; **6.** over; **7.** up; **8.** up; **9.** of, on **10.** for

6 Phrasal verbs 2: Matching definitions

1. C, **2.** H, **3.** A, **4.** G, **5.** F, **6.** D, **7.** I, **8.** E, **9.** J, **10.** B

7 Phrasal verbs 3: A quiz

1. register on arriving at a hotel, **2.** break the rules without consequences, **3.** take care of, **4.** postpone sth., **5.** arrive somewhere, **6.** become

8 Phrasal verbs and prepositions: An e-mail of application

1. for, **2.** to, **3.** in, **4.** After, **5.** at, **6.** in, **7.** in/during, **8.** in, **9.** with, **10.** for, **11.** at, **12.** in/at/of, **13.** in, **14.** for, **15.** in, **16.** for, **17.** to, **18.** from

Unit 16 Word formation (Key)

1 Common noun endings: -ance and -ence

a) **1.** to accept, **2.** (in)dependent, **3.** to differ, **4.** distant, **5.** to exist, **6.** innocent, **7.** silent, **8.** to violate
b) **1.** distance, **2.** silence, **3.** difference, **4.** violence, **5.** innocence, **6.** intelligence
c) Individuelle Schüler/innenantworten

2 Turning verbs into nouns

a) **1.** argument, **2.** competition, **3.** decision, **4.** description, **5.** development, **6.** encouragement, **7.** excitement, **8.** explanation, **9.** improvement, **10.** production
b) **1.** argument, **2.** encouragement, **3.** decision, **4.** competition, **5.** improvement, **6.** description
c) Individuelle Schüler/innenantworten

3 Turning adjectives into nouns

a) **1.** Homelessness, **2.** forgetfulness/laziness/rudeness, **3.** darkness, **4.** weaknesses, **5.** forgetfulness/laziness/rudeness, **6.** Tiredness
b) Individuelle Schüler/innenantworten

4 Negatives

a) **nouns:** disbelief
verbs: to dislike, to disagree, to misbehave, to misunderstand, to misspell, to misuse
adjectives: unexpected, unbelievable, unknown, unable, inaccurate, inappropriate, inefficient, incapable, dishonest, impossible, impolite, imperfect, impatient, illegal, illiterate, illogical, illegible, irregular, irresponsible, irrational, irresistible, careless, harmless, helpless, endless
b) **1.** dishonest, **2.** unbelievable, **3.** impolite, **4.** misunderstood, **5.** harmless, **6.** illegal

Unit 17 Relative clauses (Key)

1 Non-defining relative clauses: Famous Australians

a) **1.** Actor Hugh Jackman, who was born on 12 October 1969 in Sydney, doesn't smoke in real life and finds it very difficult to smoke in movies.
2. Singer Kylie Minogue, whose first big hit in 1989 was called "I should be so lucky", launched her own social network called KylieKonnect in 2007.
3. Media mogul Rupert Murdoch, who was a friend of US President Ronald Reagan, started with a local newspaper and expanded his empire in the UK, Asia and USA.
4. Runner Cathy Freeman, who lit the Olympic flame at the 2000 Sydney Olympics, announced her retirement from competitive running in 2003.
5. Australia's seventh Prime Minister Billy Hughes, whose nickname was "Little Digger", changed parties five times over his parliamentary career of 51 years.
6. Fictitious character Dame Edna Everage, who is played by comedian Barry Humphries, has been mentioned on *The Simpsons* three times.
b) Individuelle Schüler/innenantworten

2 Defining or non-defining relative clause?

1. a, **2.** b, **3.** a, **4.** a, **5.** b

3 The place where, the day when and the reason why

Individuelle Schüler/innenantworten

4 Contact clauses: The shortest possible form

1. The people climbing the tower are trying to get a better view.
2. The woman talking to your mother is my teacher.
3. The first speed boat I ever saw belonged to my uncle.
4. The new battery of the phone I had bought at the marktet unfortunately didn't last long.
5. The bouquet was made from flowers grown locally.
6. This is the book I was talking to you about.

Unit 18 Adverbial clauses (Key)

1 Sentence halves

a) **1.** D, **2.** G, **3.** A, **4.** B, **5.** C, **6.** I, **7.** J, **8.** E, **9.** F, **10.** H
b) They tell us when, where, how or why something happened.
c) Individuelle Schüler/innenantworten

2 Language in use: Find the correct word

0: B, **Q1:** B, **Q2:** C, **Q3:** A, **Q4:** D, **Q5:** D, **Q6:** A, **Q7:** D, **Q8:** D, **Q9:** C, **Q10:** D

3 Connecting sentences

1. The five-cent coin looks very Canadian since it has a picture of a beaver on it.
   Because the five-cent coin has a picture of a beaver on it, it looks very Canadian.
2. You need proper shoes to go hiking in the Alps since the ground is rough and hard.
   Due to the rough and hard ground, you need proper shoes to go hiking in the Alps.
3. Before my brother started medical training he had driven a lorry for a living.
   My brother drove a lorry for a living when he started medical training.
4. Although the dolphin lives in the sea it is not a fish, it's a mammal.
   The dolphin is not a fish, it's a mammal even though it lives in the sea.
5. When I was much younger, I enjoyed camping out.
   I enjoyed camping out since I was much younger.
6. American football players wear lots of protective clothing so they don't get hurt much.
   American football players don't get hurt much because they wear lots of protective clothing.
7. I took notes while I was taught to use the new accounting software.
   When I was taught to use the new accounting software I took notes.
8. Not only did Jake the ironing, he also prepared breakfast.
   Jake did the ironing and prepared breakfast.